VIOLET

MINT

PARSLEY

GREEK OREGANO

LEMON VERBENA

hyssop

RED CLOVER

RUE

SAGE

ROSEMAR

NATURE PRINTING

with HERBS, FRUITS & FLOWERS

LAURA DONNELLY BETHMANN

A Storey Publishing Book
Storey Communications, Inc.

The mission of Storey Communications is to serve our customers by publishing practical information that encourages personal independence in harmony with the environment.

Edited by Deborah Balmuth

Cover design by Meredith Maker

Cover illustration by Laura Donnelly Bethmann

Text design and production by Greg Imhoff

Photographs by Kevin Kennefick

Line drawings by Alison Kolesar

Indexed by Northwind Editorial Service

Copyright © 1996 Laura Donnelly Bethmann

Thanks to the following artists who contributed work to this book: John Doughty (p. 43); Gudrun Garkisch (p. 53); Peter Heilmann (p. 4, from his collection); Nanjo Kubota (p. 51, 57); Irmgard Lucht (p. 85); Fred Mullet (p. 30); Renata Sawyer (p. 79); Helga Wagner (p. 79). *Turkish Towel (Gigartina papillata),* on page 8 reprinted with permission from *The Leaf Book, A Field Guide to Plants of Northern California,* by Ida Geary, published in 1972 by Tamal Land Press.

Thanks to Guild Art Centre, Northampton, Massachusetts and Al's Auto Body Works, Williamstown, Massachusetts for loaning supplies for photographs.

The information in this book is true and complete to the best of our knowledge. All recommendations are made without guarantee on the part of the author or Storey Communications, Inc. The author and publisher disclaim any liability in connection with the use of this information. For additional information please contact Storey Communications, Inc., Schoolhouse Road, Pownal, Vermont 05261.

Storey Publishing books are available for special premium and promotional uses and for customized editions. For further information, please call the Custom Publishing Department at 1-800-793-9396.

Printed in Canada by Métropole Litho

10 9 8 7 6 5 4 3 2

Library of Congress Cataloging-in-Publication Data
Bethmann, Laura Donnelly, 1953–
      Nature printing with herbs, fruits & flowers / Laura Donnelly Bethmann.
            p.   cm.
      "A Storey Publishing Book."
      Includes bibliographical references and index.
      ISBN 0-88266-929-X (alk. paper)
      1. Plant prints. 2. Leaf prints. 3. Prints—Technique. I. Title.
      NE953.B48 1996
      769'.434—dc20   95-54100
                                                   CIP

CONTENTS

DEDICATION

 To the memory of my mother, Marie Donnelly

ACKNOWLEDGMENTS

In attempting to compile as much information about nature printing as possible within a limited amount of time, I have paid special attention to plant printing because it is the area of my experience. I cannot thank enough the members of the Nature Printing Society, who have contributed their own work and knowledge in their areas of expertise: John Doughty, Charlotte Elsner, Gudrun Garkisch, Ida Geary, Peter Heilmann, Dr. F. G. Hochberg, Nanjo Kubota, Irmgard Lucht, Fred Mullet, Renata Sawyer, Shingo Takahashi, Helga Wagner, and many other nature printers I have known and learned from over the years through the Society's excellent newsletter. Though separated by thousands of miles, we all share a common reverence for art and nature.

To Bertha Reppert, thank you for suggesting that I should "perhaps do a book," and for introducing me to Storey Publishing. Thanks to Deborah Balmuth, whose editorial and organizational skills have greatly benefitted this book.

I'm grateful to my friend Lori Halsey for faithfully checking up on me; my friend Susan Whelan for her careful reading and suggestions to the manuscript; my husband, Chris, for his brutally honest criticism of the first article I'd ever written and for finding time in his busy schedule to free up more of mine to work on this project; and our daughters, Kate and Cara, for their help with the children's projects and for withstanding my constant response, "… just let me finish typing one more page!"

PREFACE

He who plants a garden finds happiness.
— *Chinese proverb*

As an artist of nature, I have regarded the earth and sky and all that grows in between. For years I relied solely on painting and drawing techniques to recreate images, until I came upon the intrinsic simplicity of nature-printed images.

One day while painting by a riverside, I picked up a small leaf from the water's edge. It was covered with a reddish-brown coating from the iron-rich water. Placing the leaf on the damp paper of my watercolor, I pressed firmly with the heel of my hand, making a faint, irregular, but distinct impression on the paper. I tried brushing a small amount of thick watercolor paint on the leaf, producing lovely results. The happenchance of this first nature printing experience left a lasting impression on me.

Prints of leaves and flowers appeared in my paintings for more than a year before I found Ida Geary's book, *Plant Prints and Collages* on a library shelf, and discovered that what I had been doing was, in fact, a long-practiced art with many variations and possibilities.

I began to learn the habitats and common and Latin names of plants, which was as exciting as printing them. But even as my knowledge of plant life grew, the art of gardening remained elusive. Up until 1986, planting a few annuals and barely tending a small perennial bed had been my only gardening experience. Then, in the spring of that year, I planted some herbs a friend gave me. I began reading some of the captivating lore of herbs. Though often neglected, my little herb patch spread and blossomed. I welcomed the fragrance of herbs in the summer air. The gardener within me was awakening.

Gardening is one of the commonest occupations for self-expression. Creating a garden provides an entrance to the realm of beauty — a connection to the earth, to life, and to creativity. Gardening and nature printing make perfect companions in any season. Even when the plants in my garden lie dormant through the winter, I'm able to remoisten previously pressed plants and create freshly printed images, my everlasting *nature-printed garden.*

Strawberry · Rosemary · Cinquefoil + Sage · Thyme · Lavender · Lady's Mantle · Red Clover

CHAPTER 1

INTRODUCTION TO NATURE PRINTING

Nature printing is the process of recreating images from the natural world. It is a direct, inexpensive process that requires some practice, but no particular artistic talent. The basic principle of nature printing is:

Natural Object + Pigment + Printable Surface = Nature Print.

Little-changed from former times, this unsung, centuries-old technique has been practiced as an art, a craft, and an aid to scientific study. It yields unlimited possibilities, restricted only by the imagination and the subjects available to the individual printer.

ART, CRAFT & SCIENCE

Simple nature prints can be used to ornament correspondence, form herbariums, and illustrate nature journals and herbals. Nature printing is an art form that can be framed and displayed, but it is also a craft that can be used to decorate linens, wearables, walls, and furnishings. Moreover, nature printing is a science, as exhibited by the beautiful volumes created by herbalists, physicians, and botanists for identification or research from the thirteenth through the nineteenth centuries.

One of the very few historical accounts of nature printing, *Typographia Naturalis,* published in 1967 by R. Cave and G. Wakeman, informs us that "There is, of course, nothing very startling in the idea of nature printing . . ." In a way, this is like saying that there is nothing very startling in the occurrence of the sun rising in the morning or the appearance of stars at night. We take for granted the obvious, the everyday, and the ordinary. But, of course, there is something startling in the seemingly commonplace.

People of all ages attending my workshops gaze wide-eyed as their first nature-printed image is revealed. Lifting an inked sage or maple leaf after having pressed it to a sheet of paper is like pulling a rabbit out of a hat. The crisp form and linear veining of the leaf seem to appear like magic. Children and adults — beginners as well as seasoned nature printers — feel the excitement and wonder of anticipation as each print is unveiled from beneath the inked original. Soon, the workroom is adorned by "tabletop gardens" of beautiful plant prints and we are enchanted by the ancient art and science of nature printing.

This book focuses on methods and applications for plant printing, but keep in mind that there are nature printers producing prints of anything they can find: spider webs, rocks, shells, vegetables, feathers, woodgrain, fish, and other animals — including human beings! I've included examples of these and other nature printing applications, which illustrate the assertion of Alexis Pedemontanus in his *Book of Art and Nature* of 1557, that with nature printing "you may make gallant things, to adorn your Chamber."

A Sixteenth-Century Account of Nature Printing

Writer Alexis Pedemontanus of Milan wrote an account in his *Book of Art,* published in 1557, of a way "to make all sorts of green Leaves, that they shall appear to be naturall ... Take green Leaves, and bruise the great Veins on the backside with some wooden Pestle, then colour them with this following colour: Take common Oyl, or Linseed Oyl, or any other thing that will make a smoake, what you need, burn this in a Lamp setting an Earthen Pot over it, that it may receive all the smoake. Then collect diligently all the smoake that sticks upon it, and mix it with Oyl of liquid Vernish, and make a Tincture, and Dye the bruised side of the Leaf therewith, with a Linnen Cloath or Cotton, then lay the side that is coloured upon a double Paper, pressing it lightly down with your hand, or some Cloath, that the Paper may be Dyed. Then taking away the Leaf neatly, you shall find the Paper curiously Dyed, to every small Vein, that it will seem to be naturall; if you would have them look green, take the sharpest Vinegar, Verdigrease, Urine, of each what may suffice; boyl them, and make a green colour, and with this Dye the Paper that is formed, and in this way you may make gallant things, to adorne your Chamber ... "

THE LORE OF PLANT PRINTING

Possibly inspired by leaf fossils, nature printing is believed to be an ancient practice. By about the year 1500, this practice was noted both for its precision and its beauty, functioning both as a tool of science and as an art form. One of the few people to unify these two disciplines was Leonardo da Vinci. His manuscript *Codex Atlanticus,* circa 1500, includes the first-known written record of the process of nature printing, accompanied by a printed impression of a sage leaf.

Other written accounts from the sixteenth century describe nature printing as both a decorative art and as a way to learn about plants. The early procedure used lamp-black (soot collected from an oil lamp) mixed with oil, which was smeared onto a leaf and then pressed by hand or with a smoothing bone between two sheets of paper.

The evolution of nature printing coincided with developments in science and technology, including the emergence of the study of botany. Plants have been used to heal the sick for thousands of years. The original medical texts, called "herbals," described plants used for their medicinal derivatives, along with methods of plant preparation and prescriptions for specific ailments. Prepared

Sage leaf blackened with lampblack and dabbed with water-soluble vehicle (a mixing agent for ink). Leonardo da Vinci and other early nature printers used this technique (with oil instead of a water-soluble vehicle).

and used by physicians, herbalists, and pharmacists, herbals usually contained drawings, engravings, or nature prints for plant identification. Gradually, universities all over Europe planted physick gardens and prepared herbariums for research. During the sixteenth century, plant investigation became a subject unto itself, separate from medicine, and the science of botany was born.

The ease of hand printing a single collection of plants for an herbal or herbarium equaled its function. In 1687, J. D. Geyer assured botanists that "the most excellent picture will result" from nature printing. He described how to spread printer's inks onto leaves and flowers and press them onto paper. "This is certainly an excellent method, and extremely useful to those botanists who have no artistic talent, as by these elegant means they can prepare an herbarium themselves," wrote Geyer.

Nature Printing in America

Daniel Francis Pastorius, the cofounder of Germantown, Pennsylvania, is credited with introducing the practice of nature printing to the British colonies of North America in 1684.

As in Europe, nature printing in the colonies served as a tool for botanists and other scientists and proved an enjoyable pastime. Adventurous pioneers in the New World made nature prints of native plants by blackening them over campfires as they headed west. These trailblazers encountered many plant species, both familiar and unknown, and impressed them into their travel journals.

Another early American practitioner of nature printing was Joseph Brientnall, a friend of Pastorius, a respected merchant, and founder of the Botanical Garden of Philadelphia. Brientnall used the garden of naturalist John Bartrum as one of his plant sources for printing. His nature prints were advertised for sale at a few pennies apiece in *The Pennsylvania Gazette* and *Poor Richard's Almanac* published by his friend Benjamin

Franklin. In these ads, Brientnall claimed his prints to be "Engraven by the Greatest and Best Engraver in the Universe," a reference to God rather than himself.

A printer by trade, Benjamin Franklin was entrusted with printing paper money for several of the colonies. Realizing that the unique, natural qualities of leaf veining would prove difficult to duplicate by hand engraving, Franklin began adding leaf impressions to the backs of currency in 1739 to deter counterfeiting.

Franklin developed a nature-printing technique that allowed him to mass-produce the print of a single leaf from one casting. Although it was known that his metal plates for printing leaf impressions on currency were made from plaster casts of leaves, the exact process was a well-kept secret, and remains a mystery to this day.

Hoping to find an expedient, inexpensive method to create nature-printed books, botanists and printers experimented for the next 100 years to achieve a means of mass-producing nature prints from one metal plate as Franklin did. By the middle of the nineteenth century, techniques had evolved that made over 1,000 identical, impeccable prints from one original plant

Eighteenth-century nature print by Johann Hieronymus Kniphof, a professor of botany at the University of Mainz in Erfurt, Germany, from an herbarium published in 1734.

First Female Botanist

The first female botanist in this country, Jane Colden, was educated by her parents in the wilderness of Coldengham, New York. When Jane showed an early interest and aptitude for the study of plants, her father, Cadwallader Colden, a scientist and politician, taught her the Latin binomial system of plant naming (developed in 1737 by Carolus Linnaeus, the Swedish botanist). In the mid-eighteenth century, Jane Colden compiled a major volume describing the plants of New York and illustrated it with 340 nature-printed specimens.

impression cast in soft metal. In the wake of stormy patent disputes by rival printers and publishers in Europe, beautiful volumes of land plants, sea plants, feathers, lace, and other objects were created in France, Germany, Austria, England, Australia, and India.

Many written accounts by those suited to the practice claimed high regard for nature printing. Alexis Pedemontanus suggested in 1557 that "you may make gallant things" with nature printing. In 1786, Johann Beckmann remarked on the "utility of these impressions" saying that they preserve the appearance of plants so well as to "afford no small assistance towards acquiring a knowledge of many vegetable productions." In a lecture entitled *Nature-Printing: Its Origin and Objects* delivered to The Royal Institution of Great Britain in 1856, Henry Bradbury exclaimed, "[H]ow powerful are the results direct from Nature herself." He stated that nature printing had "come to the aid of science."

Of course, Bradbury had no way of knowing the tremendous effect that the recent, fledgling invention of photography would soon have on science — and on publishing, education, and communications. A rather simple photographic method called *cyanotype* was an early attempt of this new science to produce nature prints. In 1843, Anna Atkins began a ten-year venture making cyanotypes of seaweeds. Her work, entitled *Photographs*

of British Seaweeds: cyanotype impressions, contains 411 plates of these plants.

The invention of halftone printing in 1866 further diminished the need for nature printing. The process was completely abandoned by the scientific community with the development of color photography in 1893.

Nature Printing Today

The largest collection of early nature-printed herbaria from around the globe resides in Mainz, Germany. However, nature prints produced in the past are still being discovered in library collections, private collections, and elsewhere worldwide.

Despite its decline as a scientific tool, nature printing has stood the test of time. The last two decades have seen a revival of this ancient art form. In 1976, a few dedicated professionals, employing nature printing as an extension of their scientific work, formed the Nature Printing Society (see Appendix).

Present-day nature printers practice the art of printing from nature in very personal ways, developed by adapting traditional methods to suit their individual purposes. The number of techniques for nature printing documented over the last several hundred years continues to grow, as innovations in nature printing are developed.

CHAPTER 2

COLLECTING & PRESSING PLANT MATERIALS

If purpose, then, is inherent in art, so is it in nature also.

— Aristotle

Each season offers new choices for nature printers. The quiet, stark beauty of winter brings seed pods, leaf skeletons, dried leaves, and evergreens. Winter foreshadows the drama of the coming spring when new life gently unfolds before the warming sun.

The abundance of summer overwhelms the senses with all the printing possibilities. This is the season to collect and press plenty of hydrangea, yarrow, Queen Anne's lace, and grapevine that will last you until next year. Autumn marks the imminent return to winter with a final burst of color for us to harvest and print.

COLLECTING PLANT SPECIMENS

The places you can find sources for nature printing are limitless — from spots as convenient as a tree-lined street with chickweed and peppergrass thriving in the sidewalk cracks to the geranium pots in your kitchen window. You can purchase plants from a florist or garden center, and fruits, vegetables, and herbs from the produce market. If you or a friend has a garden, so much the better, but a nearby field or patch of woods will provide a large variety of plants, too. On a grander scale, mountains, oceans, lakes, bogs, and marshes all support interesting wildlife that can be used for nature printing. Every season offers new choices.

Turkish Towel (Gigartina papillata). This print of a marine algae, or seaweed, was done by Ida Geary, author, naturalist, teacher, and a founding member of the Nature Printing Society, for her book The Leaf Book: A Field Guide to Plants of Northern California, which contains over three hundred nature-printed illustrations.

Good Leaves for Beginners

Most tree leaves are good for beginning printers, including the following.

- Ash
- Aspen
- Beech
- Birch
- Cherry
- Cottonwood
- Dogwood

- Elm
- Ginkgo
- Hawthorn
- Hazel
- Magnolia
- Maple
- Oak

- Poplar
- Sassafras
- Sweet gum
- Sycamore
- Tulip tree
- Walnut
- Willow

Begin in Your Own Backyard

Selecting specimens from your own surroundings is an easy place to start. Choose healthy plants on a dry day after the dew has evaporated. For a beginner, leaves are preferable to flowers because they are sturdier and easier to print. In general, prominently veined or textured leaves reveal more detail when printed than smooth ones. Clip individual leaves or three- to six-inch sprigs of small leaves (handling large specimens and whole plants is discussed in Chapter 5), and put them immediately into plastic bags. Most leaves don't require pressing if you are going to print them the same day.

Field Collecting

While gathering materials on your home ground may keep you quite busy, roaming in the great outdoors will expand your possibilities. Before you start roaming, take the following precautions. Wear proper clothing and footgear, and be aware of poison ivy, poison oak, and poison sumac. Obtain a field guide of the wildflowers and plants in your region so you will recognize poisonous plants if encountered and be able to identify your newfound specimens. Attempt to contact property owners before removing plants from even seemingly remote locations. If you see lovely wildflowers growing along a roadside or in a meadow, go to the nearest house or business to find the landowner and get permission to collect plants. If in doubt, check town, county, or city records for property ownership. State and national parks don't allow removal of anything, but it doesn't hurt to ask the park superintendent, especially if you are collecting plants that are considered weeds.

Rare and endangered species should never be disturbed. Local gardens, conservation groups, or your state department of natural resources can provide a list of threatened plants.

Equipment for Field Collecting

The following items are useful to keep close at hand in your car or in your backpack for collecting specimens.

- Notebook, self-stick note pads, self-stick labels for bags, and waterproof marker.

- Scissors and/or hand pruners for cutting stems, twigs, and woody plants. If you have an interest in collecting leaves and flowers from trees, you may also need to purchase long-handled pruners.

- A trowel or small shovel for digging up plant specimens.

- Zip-seal plastic bags in a variety of sizes to store specimens.

Basic equipment for collecting plant specimens for nature printing.

- Spray bottle of water to keep specimens from wilting.

- Lightweight plant press, or, if you're traveling by car, newspapers and some weights (in a box to eliminate shifting while traveling). Delicate plants, especially, should be pressed quickly.

- Container of water for transporting cut flowers or whole plants that you want to print fresh, not pressed.

- A field guide or two describing the wild plants found in your region of the country.

- Insect repellent and sunscreen.

Record Keeping

Once you have discovered a lovely place full of wild growing things, obtained permission from the landowner to gather there, resolved not to remove any endangered plants, assembled all the necessary materials, and arrived at your chosen site on a dry, pleasant day, you're ready to begin. First write down the date and location of the site in your notebook. In addition to the town and state, mention any permanent landmarks and road names. You might want to draw a map and include the name, address, and phone number of the landowner in case you want to return to the location in the future.

Note the habitat. Is it a wild field, a marshy meadow, shady woods, a hillside, or lakeside? Mention the flower colors and fragrances, and whether they attract any bees or butterflies. Note anything of interest to you. All of this information can be used to create a nature-printed herbarium of the plants you collect (see page 74).

List the name of each plant collected. Do an initial identification of each specimen on-site, while looking at the whole plant. You can do further research at home.

Transporting Specimens

Place your collected materials in plastic bags. Inflate the bags before closing to provide a protective air cushion. (Zip the seal, leaving one or two inches open. Blow air into the opening to inflate and seal completely.)

If you can't press specimens immediately upon returning home, store them in the refrigerator. Do not leave them in plastic bags unrefrigerated. Plants that

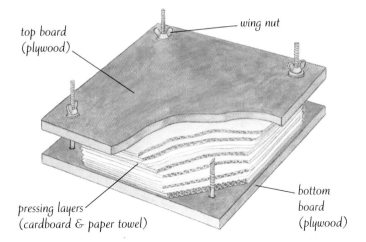

top board (plywood)
wing nut
pressing layers (cardboard & paper towel)
bottom board (plywood)

A simple plant press can easily hold several layers of specimens.

One inflated plastic bag can hold several different kinds of leaves. Just be sure to label them well.

have wilted during transport may revive in the refrigerator. I have successfully stored herbs, tree leaves, and other plants under refrigeration for one to three weeks. When collecting wildflowers, cut and transport them in a container of water or press them on site.

To collect an entire plant, dig it up with as much root as possible and gently shake off excess soil. Using a spray bottle of water, spray once or twice inside a plastic bag large enough to accommodate the plant, insert plant, close the bag, and label it.

PRESSING SMALL PLANTS

Good results in nature printing depend on well-pressed specimens. Folded, wrinkled leaves and petals produce poor nature prints. It's very important to take the time to press your specimens carefully. The simplest way to press small specimens is with an old telephone directory. Here's how to press.

1. Remove the plant from the plastic bag and brush any grit from leaves and roots with a soft artist's brush. If necessary, wash away excessive soil from roots and pat dry.

2. Open the telephone book about ½-inch from the bottom and lay the specimen flat in a natural position. If the plant is straining to spring back to its natural form, thin leaves and delicate petals can be secured with wet strips of newspaper. If the plant has dense foliage, remove a few leaves. Positioned underside-up (for texture and veining when printing), but for variation arrange a few leaves to show their top side.

3. Apply a self-stick label with the plant name and the date hanging off the edge of the page so you can read it when the book is closed.

4. Carefully cover the plant with another ½-inch thickness of pages and insert the next specimen.

5. When all the leaves are tucked inside the "telephone book press," weight the top with a couple of heavy books or a stack of magazines. Although not a professional method, using telephone books or newspapers, carefully labeled and topped with weights, works well. They can be stacked, and the label system is an easy reference.

Many plants need only a little flattening to make them easier to work with. Pressing them for a half-hour to an hour will usually be sufficient. Some plants require longer, even overnight. Sturdy plants can be stored in the press for one year or more and remoistened between damp sheets of newspaper to make them supple enough for inking (see page 14).

If you are unsure whether a plant was pressed successfully, the leaves and stems can be suitably rearranged after having pressed for fifteen to thirty minutes, until slightly slack.

Pressing Flowers

Flowers are a challenge to press. They can be difficult to ink successfully when unpressed, but after pressing they tend to fall apart while being inked. I press most flowers

Compensating for the Thick & Thin of It

Stems and branches that are thicker than the leaves must be compensated for because uneven pressing produces wrinkled leaves. To do this, arrange the plant or branch on top of several sheets of newspaper large enough to accommodate it. Prepare pads of newspaper equal to the thickness of the stem or branch, and place them over the leaves only. Secure it with tape if necessary. Lay large sheets of newspaper over the whole plant and place weight on top of it.

Certain flowers require padding to equalize the pressing. For example, daisy-like blossoms that have thin ray petals around a thick central disc need a "doughnut" of padding over the petals to match the thickness of the disc. To make one, cut a circle a little larger than the flower from a pad of newspaper the same thickness as the disc, and then cut a hole in the center the same size as the disc. Place this pad over the flower petals, then cover the whole plant with more newspaper. Press.

Carnations, roses, and many full flowers should be printed fresh, not pressed, since pressing will crush them.

This flowering dogwood print was made from the pressed petal-like bracts. The tiny buds were penciled in and painted.

for just a few minutes prior to inking and printing them. Flowers such as roses and carnations can be pressed slightly with just a bit of weight or they will crush. However, I prefer to print them without pressing.

Flowers with many parts often need to be disassembled for pressing. The iris, for example, has three erect petals at the top, called standard blades, and three lower ones, called fall blades. To prepare the iris for pressing, cut the flower at its base from the stem. Remove one standard blade and one fall blade and press them separately from the rest of the flower. The iris can then be printed without these blades altogether, as if they were absent from view, or these blades can be added to show the complete flower. (To print iris, see page 48.)

Some flowers will keep for months in a press and, when dried, can be remoistened for printing. For variety when printing flowers, try pressing them in a variety of positions, if possible, such as wide open, partly closed, and on their sides.

Sometimes, as when pressing the petal-like bracts of flowering dogwood trees, I prefer to remove the central disc that is comprised of the actual tiny flowers by cutting them away with a single edge razor blade. I then press the bracts intact. They can remain pressed for up to one year and, handled with care, remoistened slightly and printed. After printing the bracts, I pencil in the tiny flowers and paint them with watercolors (see art above).

Pressing Large, Flowering Plants

Very large plants are cumbersome to ink and print, but if they are divided into sections the plants require less space to press and are easier to handle. In the printing process, the entire plant will be reunited as you print each section and put the pieces of the "plant puzzle" back together again.

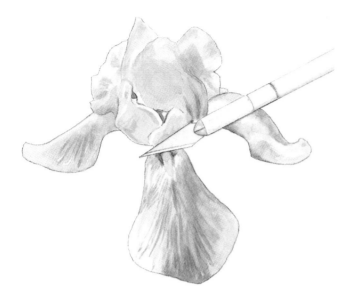

To prepare the iris for pressing, remove one standard blade and one fall blade and press them separately from the inner flower.

Begin by covering a flat surface, such as a tabletop or corner of the floor, with newspaper. I use layers of folded newspaper sections that measure 14 inches by 23 inches, and cut plants in lengths to fit within that area. Or, I remove individual or clusters of leaves from the stem and press separately. Pad particular sections of the plant when necessary to compensate for differences in thickness (as described on page 12). Stack the layers of plants between ½-inch deep sections of newspaper and press with a thick covering of newspaper topped with weight.

Use your judgment in adapting these pressing procedures. Practice will be your guide, as it is impossible to describe methods for pressing every kind of plant. Experimentation is half the fun. For example, I print the brilliant hibiscus that grows in my garden while it blooms in late summer. This plant requires no pressing at all. The leaves are flat, but because the flower petals have a slight curve, pressing them only creates wrinkles. So, as I remove a petal or leaf from a hibiscus stem, it is immediately inked, using a small brayer or dabber, and then printed. (See Hibiscus on page 46.)

Cold Pressing

Some nature printers store sturdy leaves in the freezer. If pressed, lay the leaves between sheets of damp newspaper or paper towels and place in zip-seal bags. Freshly picked leaves can be frozen loose in zip-seal bags. The frozen leaves will defrost in minutes and be ready to use for many printings. They can be stored in the freezer for up to one year. Most leaves also remain fresh for a few weeks stored in bags in the refrigerator.

Fruits and Vegetables

The leafy tops of carrots, radishes, beets, and other fresh vegetables and fruits can be removed and pressed in the same manner as other leaves are pressed. The fruit or vegetable itself is best used fresh and cut in half to reveal seeds and other inner structures. Blot well to absorb excess moisture before ink or paint is applied. Halving fruits and vegetables creates a flat surface which makes printing easier and results in interesting images.

REMOISTURIZING DRY PLANTS

Plants need to be supple to accept ink from a brayer, dabber, or brush or they will crumble. If you are using plants that were collected in autumn or winter and have become brittle, or plants that have dried in the press, you will need to soften them up before use. For this task, you will need a plastic bag, newspapers, a spray bottle of water, and weights.

Using the spray bottle, mist dried autumn or winter leaves on both sides. Spray inside the plastic bag, lightly, as well. Put the leaves inside the bag, seal it, and let them rest a few hours or overnight. Once they are pliable, they are ready to press. Dampen several layers of newspaper and sandwich the now pliable plants between the layers. Cover with a sheet of plastic or plastic bag and add weight. Most leaves will press flat within thirty minutes to an hour.

To remoisturize a dry, pressed plant, begin by placing the plant between layers of dampened newspaper, cover that with plastic, and place a weight on top. A pressing time of 30 minutes to overnight will be required, depending on the plant. Check the plant occasionally and spray the newspaper again if it becomes dry. But beware: leaving plant material in a damp press for too long encourages mold growth. Dry, pressed flowers should remain in a damp press for only a few minutes and must be handled with care.

Many flowers are too delicate to use when not fresh, although some, such as dogwood, Queen Anne's lace, lavender (in bud), and red clover, can be stored in the press for up to a year and remoisturized for use.

Skeleton Leaves. These dried winter leaves were remoisturized before being inked and printed.

... wberr ... · Rosemary · Cinquefoil + Sage · Thyme · Lav ...

CHAPTER 3

PRINTING SUPPLIES & EQUIPMENT

N ature printers use some of the traditional tools and supplies of printmakers, painters, and craftspeople, but useful supplies can also be found in pharmacies, junkyards, or auto supply stores or even lying around the house.

Nature printing lends itself to most media, so if you already have art or craft supplies, you can probably make use of them in nature printing. It is easy to get carried away with wanting to try all the wonderful art products on the market, but that can be expensive. If you are unsure of where to begin, buy only the minimum printmaking supplies needed to experiment.

Pigments

Most nature printers use block printing inks. These produce excellent results, are readily available, and come in small and large tubes and cans. They are applied to plants with a brayer, bristle brush, or dabber. Begin with just one tube of black ink or, at most, one tube each of black, white, red, yellow, and blue. Inks do not come in the wide variety of colors that professional watercolor or oil paints do, but you can mix the colors to create new colors, shades, and tints. Watercolor washes can also be added to dry prints for added color. Inks are favorable for general use and work well on paper, fabric, wood, walls, and almost any surface.

Supplies for printing with oil-based and water-based inks.

Working with Inks

Inks are either oil based or water based. To use oil-based inks for nature printing, you must add linseed oil, poppy seed oil, or other oil preparation made for printmaking, which reduces the tack (stickiness) of the ink and results in a more even application, fewer roller marks, and eas-

ier printing. Clean up oil-based inks with solvents such as kerosene or mineral spirits. Keep in mind that solvents are flammable, volatile, potentially toxic, and should be used in a well-ventilated area. Carefully follow label directions. Special hand cleaners are available for removing ink, or you can wear latex gloves.

The art materials industry, in response to user concern regarding toxic materials, has recently developed a number of products as alternatives to traditional materials. For example, Turpenoid and Aquasol are two brand names of safe solvent substitutes for cleaning tools used with oil-based paints and inks. Grumbacher Max oil colors mix and clean up with water, but are like conventional oil paints in other respects. Look for product labels marked "nontoxic" or "health label" if you have these concerns.

Many water-based inks are difficult to use for nature printing as they dry too quickly on the palette during printing sessions because they are mixed with water.

Finding Supplies

Except where noted, the materials listed in this chapter are available at art and craft supply stores, and through mail-order companies (see Appendix). If you are having trouble finding something or have questions about any product, don't hesitate to ask your local art supply dealer or call the mail-order company. Often they can help you locate the product or suggest an alternative product that will work for your project.

Graphic Chemical and Ink Company, however, has a line of water-based inks that use a water-soluble vehicle for mixing instead of water. These inks perform as well as oil-based inks do, and when dry, will not wash off, making them a good choice for use on fabric and other washable surfaces, in addition to paper. Many water-based colors are nontoxic and have no fumes. All water-based inks clean up with mild soap and water. Lava Soap, Artist's Soap, or a waterless hand cleaner removes water-based ink from hands.

The behavior of inks can be altered by adding other products. *Extender* dilutes ink color, making it more transparent. *Cobalt drier* or *Japan drier* speeds up the drying process. *Sureset* compound reduces the tack of ink for better distribution, but it also keeps ink from drying, so a drier should accompany the use of Sureset. When using a drier without Sureset, add a drop of oil of cloves (available at a pharmacy) to keep the ink mixture from drying too fast on the palette. All of these products should be added to ink in minute amounts.

Pigments Especially for Fabric

You can obtain excellent results printing on fabric from oil-based printing ink or from the Graphic Chemical and Ink Company water-based ink mentioned above. The printing process on fabric is the same as for printing on paper. Unlike fabric paints, inks never need to be heat-set. Fabric printed with inks is useable when dry, but should not be washed for four weeks following application.

There are a large variety of fabric paints on the market that adapt to nature printing, although many result in a thick, rubbery print with little detail. However, one fabric paint product with no rubbery quality is Deka Permanent Fabric Paint. This paint can be thinned with *textile extender,* applied to a plant specimen with an artists' soft or bristle brush, and then printed onto the fabric. When dry, heat-set the paint by ironing the opposite side of the fabric.

Watercolor Paint

To use tube watercolors, squeeze the paint into a small cup and thin it slightly with about an equal amount of water to create a creamy pigment that can easily be spread on plants for printing. The paint will adhere to plants more easily if they have first been coated with a mixture of one part mild liquid soap to two parts water. Use watercolor brushes to apply both the soap mixture and the paint. Paper is the only appropriate surface for printing with watercolors. American and European printmaking papers need to be dampened for nature printing, but soft, absorbent Asian papers do not.

Other Pigments

You might want to try printing with stamp pads, markers, and stamp embossing powders. Oil or acrylic paints,

Other pigments that can be used for nature printing.

sumi ink, and other printmaking media such as etching or lithographic inks are also worth trying. For indirect techniques such as rubbing, try crayons or soft colored pencils such as Prismacolor pencils.

THE PALETTE

The best palette to use for preparing oil- or water-based ink, and for inking plant specimens, is a sheet of window glass. I use a 16-inch by 20-inch sheet of glass for every four or five colors and a separate glass sheet for inking the plants. The glass is available in any size you require from a hardware store or glass cutter. The raw edges of cut glass can be a safety hazard, but a professional glass cutter can polish them for you. Some printers go to junkyards to find windows removed from old car doors, complete with safe, polished edges. A sheet of Plexiglass, a white-glazed dinner plate, a disposable paper palette, or freezer paper from the supermarket also works well. When using a clear palette of glass or plastic, place a white sheet of paper underneath to improve visibility when you're rolling out ink.

Mix watercolor paints in a plastic watercolor palette, small cups such as shot glasses, or a foam egg carton.

Palette Knives/Ink Spreaders

Palette knives are for mixing and spreading inks on the palette in preparation for rolling out with a brayer. You can also make your own disposable ink spreaders from matboard scraps cut with a utility knife into strips approximately one inch by two inches. If you don't have any matboard scraps for this purpose, ask your local picture framer or art organization — after cutting mats for pictures, they always have leftover scraps, which are often just discarded.

PIGMENT APPLICATORS

The three most common methods for applying ink and paint to printable objects require brayers, brushes, or dabbers.

Brayers

Soft rubber brayers, not hard brayers, are used for rolling ink onto the plants. Brayers come in a variety of sizes from ¼-inch long to eight inches long. Polyurethane brayers work well also. Expensive composition or gelatin brayers, available in larger sizes, are suitable only for oil-based inks.

Brushes

You will need watercolor brushes for applying watercolor paints directly to plants or embellishing nature prints with watercolor. You may also want to use bristle brushes, which are stiffer than watercolor brushes, to apply ink to plants. Flat or round brushes are available in sizes appropriate to every need. Good-quality synthetic or ox-hair blend brushes are moderately priced and do a fine job. Expensive sable brushes are not necessary for nature printing.

Dabbers

Dabbers are a traditional tool. The easiest way of obtaining suitable dabbers is to make them yourself from a variety of items, some of which you probably have around the house. Soft foam cosmetic sponges or dense foam blocks made for young children (often labeled bath blocks) are ready-to-use dabbers.

Nature printer John Doughty makes simple dabbers by fashioning a handle from a bottle cork, 35mm film roll canister, or wooden dowel (about one inch wide) and covering that with dense, adhesive-backed vinyl foam. You simply remove the top layer of clear plastic, cut the foam to fit your handle and adhere. The adhesive makes the foam easy to use, and its density provides a fine, absorbent surface for applying ink. One type of adhesive-backed vinyl foam is Camper Mounting and Sealing Tape, sold in auto parts stores.

One-quarter-inch thick sheets of continuous (not shredded) polyurethane foam, available in craft and fabric shops or carpet stores, also are good for making dabbers. Cut a foam circle about three times wider than the width of the handle you are using, wrap it around one end, and secure it with a rubber band.

Just about any elongated item will serve as a handle. Try recycling empty correction fluid, medicine, or sample-size cosmetic containers. For smaller dabbers, use flat-top clothespins, dried-up markers, or unsharpened pencils. Large dabbers can be made by covering the bottom end of plastic soda bottles of varying sizes. Use whatever items you have on hand to suit your needs.

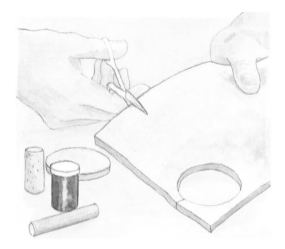

To make a dabber, begin by selecting a handle and cutting a circle of foam.

Make as many dabbers as you will need for a session of printing. The foam is disposable, although it can be cleaned and reused. If you're using a children's foam block, the dried, inked end of it can be shaved off with a single-edge razor blade to expose a new surface.

Tools used for applying pigments include: dabbers (various sizes made from foam mounted on bases of bottles, corks, and clothespins), palette knives, ink spreaders (disposable ones made from matboard scraps), soft (not hard) rubber brayers, and watercolor and bristle brushes.

PAPER

To begin, a pad of newsprint paper and a roll of sumi (kozo) paper will provide inexpensive but receptive surfaces for practice. Cut rolled paper to size as needed and tape the corners to keep it flat while working. As your control and skill in nature printing develop, you will want to invest in better quality, long-lasting papers, reserving the newsprint and sumi for test printing.

Art Paper

The wide array of art papers available makes choosing difficult. Japanese and Chinese papers are highly valued

Experiment with different types of art papers for printing.

by many nature printers for their strength and beauty. Paper was invented in China nearly two thousand years ago. The luminous, fibrous surfaces of these Asian papers are absorbent and softly exhibit the details and textures of plants. Masa and Tableau are a step up from sumi paper in quality and are not costly. White Japanese papers such as Hosho, Goyu, and Mulberry are excellent choices. Naturally colored, textured papers such as Kinwashi and Kasuiri also produce interesting results.

Popular European and American printmaking papers, such as Arches 88, Rives, and Rising, are heavier and less absorbent than Asian papers. They sometimes require more ink, dampening before printing, or greater pressure when printing. One inexpensive, good quality paper is

Incidental Supplies

- Tweezers
- Ruler or straightedge
- Scissors
- Pencils
- Kneaded and gum erasers
- Removeable tape
- Spray bottle of water
- Paper towels
- Container of water

For cleaning up water-based pigment:
- Rags or paper towels
- Water

- Mild soap
- Lava soap (for hands)

For cleaning up oil-based pigment:
- Rags or paper towels
- Solvent such as kerosene or mineral spirits
- Special hand cleaner (available at art supply stores)
- Latex gloves (optional)

Daniel Smith Archival. In addition to those mentioned above, I have also enjoyed printing with Coventry Rag, Arches Cover, Lana Gravure, Magnani Pescia, Superfine Letterpress, Cogon Grass Paper, Chiri, Yatsuo (in a variety of colors), and Evanescent Papers, among others.

To combine nature printing with watercolor painting, I use Arches (or other top quality watercolor paper) hot press (smooth surface), and cold press (slightly textured surface). However, swift brush strokes of watercolor, which is less rigorous or wet than painting, can embellish a nature print on any of the papers mentioned above.

Obtaining Desired Size

Cutting paper is the obvious way to obtain the desired size, but folding and tearing paper preserves the fibrous look of deckled edges. First, wash and dry hands thoroughly before handling paper. Even if your hands look clean, the natural oils on skin can stain or be absorbed by the paper, thereby resisting or discoloring water base pigments. Work on a clean, flat surface.

For European or American papers, fold to desired width or length making a firm crease. Be careful not to wrinkle paper. Now, open the paper and refold in the opposite direction, pressing firmly along the crease. Repeat once or twice, weakening the paper fibers along the crease each time. Open the sheet, lay it on the table, and hold one side in place with one hand. With your other hand, grip the edge of the other side, and gently pull away, tearing on the crease. Or place a ruler or straightedge on the crease and gently tear the sheet along the edge, as illustrated.

The fibers of most Japanese and Chinese papers are much longer and need to be dampened before tearing. Fold and crease once, open the sheet, quickly drag a wet watercolor brush in a straight line along the crease, and gently pull the paper apart.

Instead of using scissors to cut deckle-edged art paper, begin by folding it to the desired size and then reversing the fold several times to weaken the paper fibers along the crease. Be careful not to wrinkle the paper.

Open up the sheet, and gently pull away to tear along the crease or hold a straightedge ruler along the fold with one hand and tear along the straightedge. This technique preserves the fibrous look of deckled edges.

PAPER TERMINOLOGY

The only way to find what papers you like printing with is to try as many types as possible. In searching for art papers you will discover a variety of descriptive terms. Here are some of the more common ones that are useful to know:

- **Acid free** refers to paper that contains no "free acid," or has a pH of at least 6.5. Paper is considered neutral with a pH of 6.5 to 7.5 and thus has a longer life than paper without this designation. Paper becomes more acidic with time, so a *pH neutral* paper that is also *buffered* will be even more permanent.

- **Bast fibers** are commonly used in papers from Asia, including flax, gampi, hemp, jute, mitsumata, and kozo (the most common fiber used in Japanese paper). The term *rice paper* is a misnomer.

- **Cotton, or rag, content** refers to the amount of cotton fibers in a sheet of paper. Traditionally used in European and American papermaking, cotton fibers are very strong, creating excellent quality paper.

- **Deckle edge** is the naturally fibrous edge of handmade papers. Machine-made papers sometimes have a simulated deckle edge.

- **Gm/m²** gives the paper's metric weight in grams per square meter of space. Another weight measurement is in pounds (lbs.) per ream (500 sheets). A 140 lb. paper means that 500 sheets of it weighs 140 pounds.

- **Handmade paper** will display some irregularities, unlike mold- or machine-made paper.

- **Hot pressed, cold pressed, and rough** refer to paper surface. Hot pressed is smooth, cold pressed is slightly textured, and rough is self-explanatory.

- **Sizing** is added to paper to control its absorbency.

Printing on Papyrus

The papyrus plant served many purposes for the ancient Egyptians, the most important being a surface on which to write. The classical cultures of the world used it for writing, as well. Thinly sliced reeds of the papyrus plant, pounded and pressed together, form a layered sheet. This paperlike material was invented much earlier than paper but is still available today (see Appendix) and makes an interesting surface for nature printing.

- **Water leaf** refers to paper with no sizing, resulting in very absorbent paper.

- Other papers to keep in mind are typing paper, stationery, and envelopes for nature printed correspondence. Illustration board, mat board, and museum board are thick paper products also receptive to nature printing.

PRESSING TOOLS

Our versatile, tactile hands are the most readily available printing tool. Pressure from the heel of the hand, or thumbs and fingers, applied to an inked plant in contact with a printing surface will transfer ink from the plant to that surface. Other tools for pressing, tamping, rubbing, or rolling by hand are large, flat spoons, printmaker's barens, clean brayers, dowels, and rolling pins. If you have access to a flat-bed printing press, use it for nature printing. Or make a "walking" printing press that uses the weight of your whole body — the second-best thing to a professional printing press.

How to Make a "Walking" Press

A "walking" printing press does not require any special supplies, just a sheet of plywood, a felt blanket, a sheet of newsprint, and printmaking paper.

1. Find a sheet of plywood larger than the plants you plan to print. For most prints, a 2-foot by 3-foot sheet is adequate.

2. Lay half of the felt blanket on the plywood leaving the rest to double over the top layer. Then place a sheet of newsprint on the blanket to keep it clean.

3. Large or generally unwieldy plants should be laid inked-side up on the newsprint in the press, with the printmaking paper then positioned face down on top. Small or easy-to-handle inked plants can be laid inked-side down on printing paper, which is then set on the press.

4. Over the plants and printing paper, lay another sheet of newsprint, and cover all with the remaining part of the blanket.

5. The press is ready for walking. With or without your shoes on, baby-step along the blanket to distribute your weight over the inked plants and paper sandwiched inside. (Note: Layers of newspaper can be used instead of blankets. This method can also be used for printing on fabric and other surfaces.)

CHAPTER 4

BASIC NATURE PRINTING METHODS

———❦———

To paraphrase the American Heritage Dictionary, art is the human effort to imitate or supplement nature by employing a set of principles and methods. Art is not some daunting, alien reality, separate from everyday life. Human beings have been creating art since the beginning of our time here on earth. After the necessities of food, shelter, and companionship were assured, art was next on the list of human pursuits. In our bewildered awe of nature all these many millennia, we have been developing ways of recreating the beauty and splendor of the earth and the heavens. The ancient art of nature printing is one of the most direct methods of imitating the images and sensations of our world, by using the objects of Nature herself.

THE PRINTING PROCESS

The basic procedure for nature printing is a simple direct printing process. A pigment-covered natural object is pressed onto paper or another receptive surface, revealing an immediate, delicately textured, life-sized image of itself. Not quite as easy as it sounds, however, nature printing takes practice to master, especially if you aren't used to working with artists' tools and materials such as inks and paints.

It is also possible to employ indirect printing processes for producing nature prints. For example, a cast made from a natural object can be inked and printed, or an impression can be made by applying pigment to paper that is covering a natural object. A few of the nature prints shown in this chapter were created using an indirect process, although all of the step-by-step projects I describe use the direct printing process.

Before you begin nature printing, keep in mind one important aspect of making art: mistakes are going to occur. Even though errors simply indicate experimentation, many of us are afraid to make them. But the only real risk involved is in acquiring knowledge about how *not* to do something. More importantly, mistakes are a crucial part of learning and should be recognized as such.

Be assured that Leonardo da Vinci made mistakes, Albert Einstein made mistakes and so did Thomas Edison. In fact, they made a lot of them. Highly creative people make more mistakes than anyone else because they have more ideas and are willing to try them out. And sometimes, erring opens doors to new, previously unthought-of developments and discoveries. Remember that mistakes are not failures; they are simply part of the learning process. Don't give up, just keep trying. Edison admitted that, "Sticking to it is the genius!"

LEAF STAMPING

The simplest introduction to the pleasures of nature printing is using a stamp pad and a leaf. Once inked on the stamp pad, the leaf can be used just like a rubber stamp to ornament letters, cards, envelopes, labels, invitations, giftwrap, or other paper surfaces.

To do leaf stamping, you will need the following materials:

- Typing paper (or any paper you choose)
- Well-inked stamp pads in your choice of colors
- Tweezers
- Leaves

Stamp pads come in a variety of colors and styles. Embossing stamp pads are available that use powder and a heat source to heighten the image and make it glisten. You can also use wide-tip or brush-style markers instead of a stamp pad (see page 30 for directions).

For plant materials, choose flat leaves that are no bigger than your stamp pad. They should be sturdy but soft, with some texture. Stamp pad ink adheres especially well to downy leaves such as sage, lamb's ear, dusty miller or geranium, but many other kinds give good results, as well. It isn't necessary to flatten the leaves in a press if you use them immediately after cutting.

You can make several prints with the same leaf. Leaves that readily absorb ink don't need to be reinked each time.

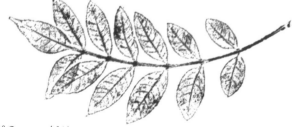

Leaf Stamped Wisteria

Step-by-Step Leaf Stamping

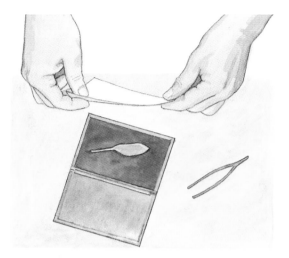

1. Lay the leaf underside down (the side where the veins are more pronounced and the texture is more evident) onto the stamp pad.

2. Cover the leaf with a small piece of paper to keep ink off your fingers and press all around, feeling the leaf through the paper. Lift the leaf to check that some ink is adhering to it, though it shouldn't be completely covered with ink or the leaf's texture will not appear when it is stamped.

3. Carefully remove the leaf from the stamp pad with tweezers.

4. Lay the leaf inked-side down on printing paper. Cover it with another piece of paper and press with the heel of your hand. If the leaf is large, hold it in place with the thumb of one hand while pressing all around with the other hand. If the print lacks detail, your leaf may have absorbed too much ink. To get rid of excess ink, press the leaf on a piece of scrap paper a few times. If the image doesn't improve, use a fresh leaf.

Alternative Inking Technique

In place of a stamp pad, you can use felt-tipped markers to ink the leaf. Both wide-tipped and brush-style markers work well.

1. Place a leaf underside up on a sheet of newspaper. Anchor the base of the leaf stem with a finger, while you color the leaf with a marker, working up from the base to the tip several times in the same direction (*not* back and forth).

2. Place the inked leaf underside down on a sheet of paper and press with the heel of your hand, as described for leaf stamping. Leaves inked with markers tend to dry quickly, so work fast.

Once you've mastered the basic technique, try inking a leaf with two or three different-colored markers and then blending the colors with a moist (not dripping wet) artist's brush before printing.

Leaf stamped using felt tipped markers

Nature-Printing with Rubber Stamps

Nature printer Fred Mullet makes his own line of rubber stamps fashioned from actual nature prints. Ranging from a small one inch ginkgo leaf to a nine and a half inch steelhead fish, Fred sells his rubber stamps and uses them to teach the arts of rubber stamping and thermography (see Appendix).

In thermography, an image is stamped with slow drying, opaque ink and then sprinkled with embossing powder. A heat gun (or other heat source) is then used to melt the powder and create a raised, shiny surface of color that gives dimension to the stamped image. These striking images are fun to make and can be further enhanced with colored markers and pencils.

Rockfish, by nature printer Fred Mullet.

Make Your Own Leaf-Stamped Stationery

*L*eaf stamping is an easy way to decorate letters, memos, post cards, envelopes, and checks. The design possibilities are endless for invitations, place cards, note cards, newsletters, holiday cards, labels, and giftwrap.

The advent of the computer and so many present-day communication options is making the art of letter writing obsolete, but, even if you never pick up a pen, you can still use your own hand-printed stationery in your computer printer and for faxing.

Project Materials

- Stamp pads (colors of your choice)
- Tweezers
- Variety of small leaves
- Typing paper, copier paper, or stationery of your choice
- Envelopes to fit selected paper

Method: By inking a leaf on both sides it is easy to print matching stationery and envelopes at the same time. This technique is applicable to other nature-printed artwork as well — just ink both sides of a leaf whenever you're making a print and you can create two prints at once. Stamp pad embossing inks and powders create glossy, raised designs that look very professional.

1. Using a stamp pad and tweezers, ink several small leaves on both sides. Turn each leaf once or twice while pressing it on the stamp pad to ensure enough ink has adhered.

2. Arrange the inked leaves on a piece of stationery as you would like them to print.

Leaf stamps can be used just like rubber stamps to ornament stationery, cards, envelopes, labels, and invitations.

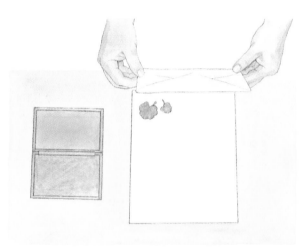

3. Position an envelope face down over the leaves on the stationery as you would like it to be printed and press with the heel of your hand (as described on page 34).

4. Remove envelope and leaf carefully and allow printed paper to dry before using.

BASIC DIRECT PRINTING

The basic direct printing method uses much the same procedure as leaf stamping, with different pigments and applicators. For this process, you need a clear work space, such as a large table, in a well-lit area where you can keep all materials close at hand.

I recommend using Graphic Chemical water-based block printing ink and water-soluble vehicle. (See Appendix for supplier address.) The Grapic Chemical water-based inks are made to be used with a water-soluble vehicle. The vehicle is a mixing agent that keeps the ink fluid and workable on the palette for hours, even days. These inks do not mix with water as other water-based inks do; water is only used for cleanup. You can use another brand of water-based ink, but be aware that inks that mix with water instead of vehicle are more difficult to work with.

Oil-based printing inks perform similarly to Graphic Chemical water-based ink, except that they use oil as a mixing agent and require solvents for cleanup. If you choose to use a different brand of ink, you should adapt the following directions as necessary (see description of supplies on page 18).

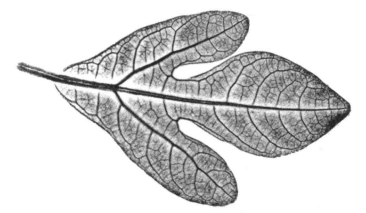

The basic direct printing method uses printing inks to capture pressed plants and flowers in amazing detail.

For basic direct printing you will need the following materials:

- Water-based block printing inks (such as Graphic Chemical brand)
- Water-soluble vehicle (such as Graphic Chemical brand)
- Soft rubber brayers in assorted sizes and/or bristle brushes and dabbers
- Palette (sheet of glass)
- Palette knife or ink spreaders
- Tweezers
- Paper for practice printing, such as newsprint or sumi paper
- Printmaking papers
- Water
- Mild liquid soap
- Paper towels
- A variety of pressed leaves and plants

For further experimentation, you might want to try using some of the following materials as well:

- Variety of papers and other surfaces for printing
- Variety of water-based and oil-based pigments
- Natural objects (other than leaves and plants) for printing
- A walking press (see page 25)

Step-by-Step Basic Direct Printing

Prepare for printing by setting up a clear work area and assembling all of your materials within easy reach. Be sure to have a practice sheet of newsprint or sumi paper ready.

Inking

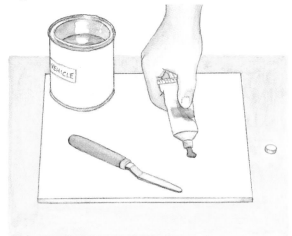

the ink to just coat the brayer — you do not need to apply heavy pressure.

Slightly widen and lengthen the ink by rolling the brayer back and forth, thinning it out, and obtaining even distribution on the brayer. The ink should be very tacky and shiny; if it feels dry and looks dull, add another drop of vehicle. Don't add too much or the ink won't dry and your print may remain sticky for weeks.

A very thin layer of ink is optimal for successful printing. If your ink layer is still heavy after rolling, scrape some off with the spreader. When the ink is an even, translucent film on the palette, you are ready to ink the leaf.

1. To ink palette, squeeze a ¼-inch blob of ink near the top edge. Place the tip of a palette knife or ink spreader in the middle of the ink and draw it straight down the palette, making a thin smear about 3 or 4 inches long.

2. Dip the corner of a clean spreader into the can of vehicle and mix a few drops of it into the ink smear with the same downward-drawing motion for several seconds. Lay the spreader at the top of the palette.

3. Select a sturdy, flat leaf. Choose a brayer to accommodate the size of the leaf. Roll the brayer back and forth along the ink smear on your palette, allowing

4. Lay the leaf underside up on a clean area of the glass and roll the inked brayer gently over it from stem to tip. Roll the brayer over the ink on the palette again to get an even layer of ink on it and reink the leaf a second time, and perhaps a third. The leaf should now be sufficiently coated.

The object itself and the printing surface determine how much ink is needed; some require less ink, while others need more. Experimentation is key in determining what works best. Your judgment will improve with practice. The only way to tell for sure is to make a print.

Printing

The most readily available printing tools are our hands. By feeling the structure of the plant beneath the thin paper covering with your fingertips, you also absorb tactile knowledge about the plants you're printing, almost without realizing it.

5. Carefully, lift the leaf by the stem with tweezers, position it over the paper, and place it inked-side down. To avoid spotting or smearing, the leaf should not be moved once it touches the paper.

6. Cover the leaf with a piece of newsprint or paper toweling (Bounty brand paper towels will not leave texture marks on prints). If you prefer to see the leaf

Alternative Ink Application Methods

If you are using a bristle brush instead of a brayer, work the brush back and forth through the ink and vehicle to charge the bristles with a moderate amount of ink. Then brush the leaf surface gently from the center to the edges until evenly coated.

If you are using a dabber instead of a brayer, you need to alter the application motion accordingly. Begin by spreading ink and vehicle with an ink spreader over the palette in a slightly thicker coat than needed for a brayer. Using a dabber, dab into the ink layer. Dab off excess ink on a clean area of the palette. Then, using some pressure, dab ink all over the leaf until a thin, even coating of color appears.

while you press it, cover with a piece of sturdy plastic such as a clear freezer bag. Cut plenty of cover sheets a little larger than your plant to have on hand during your printing session.

7. Press with your hands. For a small leaf, press with the heel of your hand. For a large leaf, press your left thumb (or right thumb, if you are left-handed) firmly at the center of the leaf to anchor it, then use the thumb, fingers, or heel of your other hand to successively press all around the leaf, radiating from the center outward to the edges and feeling the leaf's structure under the sheet of paper. Be careful not to shift the leaf. You can also try a gentle rubbing motion. The body of the leaf is more likely to adhere to the paper than the stem is, so press the body of the leaf first, the stem last.

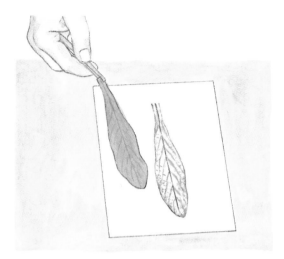

8. Slowly, remove the paper covering. Wipe the ink off the end of the tweezers, then grasp the stem of the leaf and lift it straight up and off the print. Lay the leaf on the glass, ready to ink again.

9. Mix more ink as needed and try printing in a variety of colors; experiment with other leaves, flowers, and whole plants.

10. Lay prints in a row to air dry thoroughly for 1 to 4 weeks before storing, mounting, or framing.

Cleanup

11. Soak brayers in a sink of soapy water for one or two minutes, then wipe ink off with a sponge, rinse, and dry. Soak brushes in a glass of soapy water (do not immerse handle) for one or two minutes, wipe off ink, rinse well under running water, and lay horizontally to dry.

12. Clean foam dabbers by successively pressing them on scrap paper until most of the excessive ink is removed. Save to reuse for future printing sessions with same ink color.

13. Scrape excess ink from glass palette. Spray palette with water, let stand a minute, and wipe clean. If you are planning to print again the next day, just

Alternative Printing Methods

Hands, arms, and shoulders can tire from a long printing session. With some objects, you may need greater pressure. There are several alternatives to printing with hand pressure. You may find one of the following methods useful.

Tamping. Use anything, from the curved underside of a large spoon to a printmaker's baren, to press or rub the image from inked plants onto a receptive surface.

Rolling. Try rolling a clean brayer, wooden dowel, or rolling pin over the paper covering your inked plant, pressing down as you roll.

"Walking." Recycle an unwanted book or telephone directory with pages that are larger than the paper you are printing on. Open the book in the center and place your printing paper on the page. Carefully lay the inked plant into position on the printing paper (inked-side down). Lay clean newsprint on top of the plant and gently close the book.

Place the book on a smooth floor or firm carpet, take off your shoes if desired, and walk on the book, shifting your feet slowly across the surface to distribute your weight over the inked plant sandwiched inside. The added pressure of this method usually defines plant images with greater clarity, so you might want to use less ink.

Place the book on your work table, open it carefully, and remove the print. Lift the cover sheet and gently grasp the plant with tweezers. Walking is also the preferred method for producing large prints (see page 25).

Flat bed printing press. If you have access to a printing press, by all means experiment with it for making nature prints. With such great pressure, your plants require only the slightest application of ink.

cover the inked palette with plastic wrap or place small cups or jar lids over leftover blobs of ink to keep them dust free.

14. Leftover ink can be covered with a loose-fitting lid or plastic wrap and stored for future use.

Tips for Better Direct Prints

- Use one glass sheet for rolling out inks and a separate glass sheet for inking plants.

- Be attentive to the condition of your plant source. Fragile plants and flowers can be printed only once or twice and require practice because they can be more difficult to work with, while some leaves and plants can be printed five, ten, or even twenty times before they begin to deteriorate. After use, store these flat in a telephone book or other press for reuse.

- Clean hands and tweezers frequently to avoid smudging.

- Clean brayers, palette knives, brushes, dabbers, and other equipment after each printing session to maintain good working order. Be prepared to clean your palette and rollers during a printing session if you have a build-up of plant debris.

Troubleshooting Ink Prints

If print is:	Try using:
Heavy-looking with little detail.	A thinner application of ink.
Spotty and/or pale.	More even pressure or more ink.
Smeared or blurred.	Extra care when positioning or pressing object.

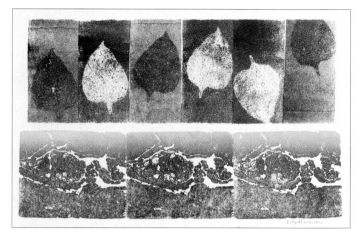

To produce the multiple colors in **Sunrise**, one leaf was printed six times across the top, alternately adhered to and removed from the inked brayer. Below, a knot in a block of wood was rolled with a brayer inked with three colors and printed three times.

Advanced Direct Printing Techniques

To start, try printing with just one color ink, according to the directions for direct printing. After you've had some practice, experiment with multiple colors and alternative ink application methods. Here are a few techniques to try.

Color Variations

- Paint the protruding veins of a leaf with a contrasting color from the leaf body. To do this, after inking the underside of the leaf with one color, gently roll a brayer inked with a different color over only the veins of the leaf before printing the entire leaf.

- Apply a thin wash of one or more watercolor paints to add color and depth to a finished print once the ink has dried.

- Experiment with combining colors by smearing and then rolling two or three colors side by side on your palette to fit the width of a 3½-inch (or larger) brayer. Roll the brayer back and forth until an even film appears showing each distinct color.

Make a Nature Journal

Direct nature printing is a wonderful tool for creating a nature journal — a daily or seasonal record of your observations and reflections on natural occurrences. Whether you live in the city, a suburban neighborhood, a small town, or on a farm in the country, there is plenty to observe (and print) in your natural surroundings.

Keeping a personal nature journal helps hone your observational skills and provides an avenue for cataloging your nature prints of plants. Along with your prints, try recording whatever else you encounter on these travels, hikes, or walks through the woods or right in your own backyard. Each season offers different stages of growth and life forms to examine.

For inspiration, you might want to refer to *The Country Diary of an Edwardian Lady* and *The Nature Notes of an Edwardian Lady* written in the early twentieth century by Edith Holden, who was a gifted observer of nature and a talented artist. She recorded her views of the English countryside, including the dates of eclipses of the sun and moon, sightings of birds, butterflies and wildflowers, the verse of her favorite poets, and much more.

If you are a gardener, your journal might include garden plans, chores, times and methods of propagation, planting and harvesting, and a pocket to keep track of receipts and expenses. If you belong to a garden or nature club, creating a journal can be a fun group project.

For more ideas on journals, see pages 74–77.

Project Materials

- A hardbound or spiral-bound blank book (available at bookstores and art supply stores).*

- In place of a blank book, use a ring binder filled with photocopying paper (or any paper you wish), punched with holes along one edge.

Nature printing opens up many creative ways of using a journal.

- Inking and printing supplies for basic direct printing method (see page 32)

*Notesketch, made by Bienfang, is a good spiral-bound book. The paper is thinner than in hardbound books, but each page is half-lined and half-blank allowing for both writing and nature printing.

Method: Nature journal writing and assembly is personal and open to many variations. A good way to begin is to take a short walk and collect interesting plants and other natural objects you find along the way.

1. Take a nature walk, gathering plants and other natural materials, and writing your observations about the day in your journal as you go along.

2. When you get home, make prints of the specimens you collected in your journal, using the basic direct printing method.

3. Use nature guidebooks and other sources to identify each print and search for interesting bits of information about it. Record these facts, quotes, and thoughts in your journal near the print.

Ink Application

- Try inking leaves and plants on both sides, then using a folded sheet of paper, create a double print.

- Make an indirect print as a result of your direct print. The negative image left on the brayer after inking a leaf can be rolled onto a printing surface, thus creating an indirect print. Another way to capture this image is to roll a large, clean brayer over an already-inked object and then roll it on a printing surface. This method works best with the very sensitive composition brayers and polyurethane brayers, although soft rubber brayers also work.

- Make a negative silhouette of a leaf by placing it on printing paper and rolling a large inked brayer over it.

- The brayer offers many different image possiblities. Try experimenting with layering, overlapping, and combining brayer-produced prints with other nature printing techniques (see Chapter 5) to create complex images.

Several colors of watercolor paints can be blended slightly on a leaf to create varigated effects when printed.

WATERCOLOR PRINTING

Watercolor paint does not produce the consistently detailed prints obtainable with ink. For some objects, such as fruits and vegetables, watercolor paint is the most suitable medium. But, as you can see from the example, the effect is more ethereal and less predictable than inks. Unless you are experienced with the use of watercolors, I recommend practicing printing techniques with inks first.

More demanding than ink, watercolor dries quickly so you need to work fast. Sized printmaking and watercolor papers must be dampened to accept watercolor painted plants and other natural objects. Begin by practicing with sumi paper and other absorbent Japanese papers that don't require dampening.

To begin watercolor printing you will need the following materials:

- Tubes of watercolor paints

- A watercolor palette (or several shot glasses or a Styrofoam egg carton)

- Soft watercolor artist's brushes

- Practice paper (sumi or another absorbent Japanese or Chinese paper)

- Printmaking or watercolor paper

- Mild liquid soap and water

- Spray bottle of water

- Paper towels

- Blotters (optional, as paper towels can serve as blotters)

- Tweezers

- A dish, sheet of glass, or other flat, washable surface for "painting" plants

Step-by-Step Watercolor Printing

1. Squeeze a small amount of watercolor paint into a palette cup. Add about an equal amount of water and mix with a brush until the paint is the consistency of cream. In another cup, combine about ½ teaspoon of liquid soap with 1 tablespoon of water and stir.

2. Place a leaf underside-up on your flat painting surface and brush on a very thin coating of the soap mixture. This will help the paint adhere to the plant.

3. Immediately brush the leaf with a coating of watercolor paint. When watercoloring a large plant, a slight spray from the water bottle may be needed just before printing to remoisten the fast-drying paint. Or, just before printing, paint over any area of the leaf that has dried.

4. Working quickly, carefully lift the leaf by the stem with tweezers, position it over the printing paper, and place it inked-side down. To avoid spotting or smearing, the leaf should not be moved once it touches the paper.

5. Cover the leaf with a piece of newsprint or paper toweling (Bounty brand paper towels will not leave texture marks on prints).

6. Press with your hands. For a small leaf, press with the heel of your hand. For a large leaf, press your left thumb (or right thumb, if you are left-handed) firmly at the center of the leaf to anchor it, then use the thumb, fingers, or heel of your other hand to successively press all around the leaf, radiating from the center outward to the edges and feeling the leaf's structure under the sheet of paper. Be careful not to shift the leaf. You can also try a gentle rubbing motion. The body of the leaf is more likely to adhere to the paper than the stem is, so press the body of the leaf first, the stem last.

7. Slowly, remove the paper covering. Wipe the ink off the end of the tweezers, then grasp the stem of the leaf and lift it straight up and off the print. Lay the leaf on the flat painting surface, ready to paint and print again.

Using Sized and Watercolor Papers

Sized printmaking paper and watercolor paper need to be dampened before printing. Begin by dampening sheets of blotter or paper towel with a few misty squirts from a spray bottle. Stack all the sheets of printing paper you intend to use by alternating each sheet with a dampened paper towel or blotter. Place the stack in a plastic bag and place a heavy book or two on top. Let the stack stand while you prepare the paints and other materials, which will take twenty to thirty minutes. The paper will absorb moisture and the weight of the books will keep it from buckling.

The paper is ready to use when it is slightly limp and evenly damp but not glistening with wetness. As you experiment and practice, your judgment in determining the right amount of moisture for your chosen paper will improve.

Make your prints on the dampened paper, according to the preceding instructions, and sandwich each print when completed between a dry paper towel or a blotter with weight on top to keep damp paper from buckling. As each print is made, place it on top of the previous print (with toweling in between), creating a stack of drying prints. Stacked prints will dry faster in a warm location. If prints are still damp the next day, change blotters and replace weights for another day or two.

To prepare sized printmaking paper or watercolor paper for nature printing, stack them between sheets of dampened paper towels, place stack inside a plastic bag, and let stand with a weight on top for up to 30 minutes.

Troubleshooting Finished Watercolor Prints

If print is:	Try using:
Heavy-looking with little detail.	Less paint or thinner paint.
Spotty and/or pale.	Thicker, more even distribution of paint, damper paper, or remoisten paint just before printing.
Smears or blurs.	Paper that is not so wet or more care when printing.

Tips for Better Watercolor Prints

- Watercolor paint will dry in the palette cups over time. Cover the cups with plastic wrap between uses, or, if dried, add a few drops of water, let stand several minutes, and mix.

- Recycle smeared or blurred prints by printing over them a second time using bright or dark colors. The sharp, clear prints of the second printing will appear to be in the foreground, while the blurred prints will seem to fade into the background.

- Experiment with using two or three colors, blending them slightly on the plant with a brush before printing.

- Combine inked and watercolor nature-printed images on a single print.

- Use watercolor washes on finished, dry prints to add depth and more color.

Make a Series of Vegetable Prints

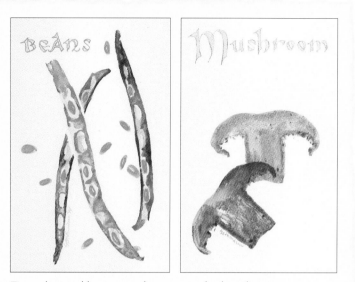

Framed vegetable prints make attractive kitchen decorations.

Small vegetable prints make a nice decorative accent hanging in the kitchen, or lovely housewarming gifts. The prints shown were designed to be matted and framed. Experiment with a variety of vegetables to create your own unique series of prints. For more information on this method of printing, see "Fruits and Vegetables" on page 48.

Project Materials

- Watercolor paints
- Watercolor brushes
- Watercolor palette
- Container of water for rinsing brushes
- Printmaking paper*
- Newsprint for making test prints
- Pencil
- Ruler
- 8-inch by 10-inch mats (optional)
- Fresh green beans, mushrooms, or other vegetables of your choice

* Daniel Smith Archival paper was used for the *Beans* and *Mushroom* prints shown. This paper must be dampened slightly to accept watercolor nature printing. See page 39 for directions. You may also use soft Japanese paper.

1. To begin, cut your printmaking paper into 8-inch x 10-inch pieces. Prepare several sheets for multiple prints.

2. Using a pencil and ruler, measure and draw a 3⅝-inch by 5⅝-inch vertical rectangle in the center of each rectangle for an 8-inch by 10-inch mat with a 3½-inch by 5½-inch opening; adjust the measurements for another size mat.

3. Prepare the mushrooms by slicing them in half lengthwise. Separate green beans by opening the seams and removing the seeds. These vegetables shouldn't need blotting, but if you use juicier ones like peppers or onions you will need to blot them.

4. Prepare watercolor paints according to the directions on page 39. It is not necessary to use the soap mixture on cut vegetables.

5. To print the bean, apply paint to the inner edges of a halved bean and make a test print on newsprint. Slightly dampen the printmaking paper, apply more paint to the bean, and position it within the pencilled area of your paper, as desired. Place it down carefully and press gently all along the bean with your fingertips. Lift it off the paper. After the paint has dried, pencil in the little seeds and paint them with a brush.

6. For the mushroom print, paint the flat side of the cut mushroom, position it over the damp paper as described for the bean and print it.

7. Label your prints with calligraphy or lettering, if desired.

CHAPTER 5

SPECIALIZED NATURE PRINTING TECHNIQUES

There is no single correct method for nature printing. Every plant or natural object has characteristics unique unto itself or to its family that present challenges to the printer. Part of the fun of nature printing is the discovery that happens along the way as you explore the possibilities of printing a wide variety of different specimens. This is the process that keeps me, and other nature printers, printing. This chapter describes some of the discoveries I've made in experimenting with printing plants and other natural objects. You can use these techniques as a starting place for developing your own ways, and for applying nature printing techniques to a variety of textured objects, both natural and man-made.

PRINTING WHOLE PLANTS & LARGE SPECIMENS

Large and complex flowering plants present particular challenges and difficulties for the nature printer, and you must use your judgment and imagination in determining how to print each plant as you're presented with it. The following step-by-step description of my procedures for printing stork's-bill, hibiscus, and iris demonstrate some of the diversity of techniques and adaptability necessary to achieve success in printing these specimens. But, remember that every nature printer has her or his own way of working. You may discover other techniques that work well for you. Nature printing is never an assembly-line process.

Stork's-bill

A few years ago, I dug up a few stork's-bill plants I found growing wild in my backyard and added them to my garden. This hardy little fernlike member of the geranium family grows six to twelve inches high, brings an abundance of tiny purplish-pink blossoms in spring, then flowers sporadically throughout the summer. The prints I made of this plant involved a couple of days' effort.

Before beginning, I assembled the following materials:

- Water-based block printing inks (such as Graphic Chemical brand)
- Water-soluble vehicle (such as Graphic Chemical brand)
- 3-inch brayer
- 1-inch brayer
- Small dabbers
- ½-inch artist's bristle brush
- 1 sheet Tableau printmaking paper

Stork's-bill I. *This print was made with the basal leaves intact.*

- Newsprint
- Single-edge razor blade
- Tweezers
- Ink spreaders
- Glass palette
- Sureset compound
- Cobalt drier
- Walking press
- Flowering stork's-bill plants
- Newspapers and heavy books (for pressing)

Preparation for Printing

The day before printing, I chose a whole plant and dug it up roots and all. I gently shook off the soil and removed the yellowed leaves. Stork's-bill has basal leaves that are quite thick at the center and a taproot that is wide at the top where the rosette of leaves emerges. I severed the root from the rosette with a sharp single-edge razor blade. I then sliced the rounded top of the root, which was about ¼-inch wide, in half lengthwise for ease in pressing and printing. The roots were then pressed between layers of newspaper with a heavy book on top.

The stork's-bill fruit are beaked capsules (from which the plant derives its common name) that grow from the axil of the leaves. I removed these and pressed them separately. The leaves radiating from the thick center of the rosette are thin and delicate. I left these intact and lay the basal leaves on a stack of newspapers, arranged in a natural looking manner. To accommodate the difference between the thick rosette and the thin outer leaves, I cut a hole in the center of a ¼-inch stack of newspaper and place it over the plant to equalize the thickness (see page 12). That was topped with another layer of newspapers and heavy books and left to press overnight.

The next day I was ready to print. I picked several stork's-bill flowers from the garden and pressed them between weighted layers of newspapers. While they pressed, I readied the inks and paper.

Printing

My walking printing press was set up with a 2-foot by 3-foot sheet of plywood, two layers of soft felt blanket, and several sheets of plain newsprint (see page 25 for directions).

To achieve the desired colors, I used one part yellow, two parts blue, and a touch of white mixed with an ink spreader and some vehicle to make a dark green. For the yellow, I then mixed yellow ink with a touch of white and vehicle. For the reddish-brown areas of the plant, I squeezed out a bit of red ink. Finally, for the purplish-

Using a Dabber

Dabbers perform in a way that brayers and brushes cannot. Inking whole plants with overlapping stems, leaves, and flowers requires a smaller or softer applicator to reach crevices of the layered, pressed plant. A soft dabber is just right for gently depositing ink in tiny nooks and crannies, and for applying ink to dried or delicate plants and flowers which are prone to crushing from a stiff brayer or harsh bristle brush. Small dabbers are also perfect for adding bits of color here and there. (See page 20 for picture of dabber and directions for making your own.)

pink color I mixed red with a small amount of blue and a touch of white and vehicle.

To begin inking, I placed the now flat rosette of leaves on a glass palette and rolled green ink onto most of the leaf area with a 3-inch brayer. With a 1-inch brayer, I added yellow to the uninked leaves and to some of the leaves inked in green. Yellow and red were then added to areas the brayers could not cover by using small foam dabbers and a bristle brush. When some of the tiny, delicate flower petals stuck to the dabber, I added a bit of Sureset Compound and cobalt drier to the purplish-pink ink, thus reducing its tackiness.

Once satisfied with the ink coverage, I laid the plant inked-side up on a sheet of newsprint in the prepared walking press, carefully arranging the leaves with tweezers. The fruits were inked with a dabber and laid inked-side up in the appropriate place with the rest of the plant on the press. A sheet of Tableau printmaking paper was placed in position over the plant. I covered this with another sheet of clean newsprint and a felt blanket, and then walked over the whole surface in my stocking feet.

Alternative Method

When this first print was successful, I decided to make another from a different point of view. Instead of printing an overhead view of the plant looking down into the rosette, I wanted to show a side view, including the roots.

To begin, I laid a sheet of Masa paper on the walking press. The stork's-bill plant from the first print was limp and unable to withstand a second inking, so I clipped over a dozen leaves from another pressed rosette and inked each one in the same manner as before. I then arranged them, one at a time, inked-side down on the sheet of Masa. The fruits and flowers were inked with the brayer and dabbers and positioned at the top of the leaves in their natural place. Roots were inked with the brayer and dabbers, and laid below the leaves. Covering all with newsprint and the blanket, I took a short "walk" over the surface.

Stork's-bill II. This print is a side view of the plant; the leaves were removed and printed singly.

Hibiscus

The bright magenta hibiscus in my garden blooms from late summer through early fall. It grows three to five feet tall, and the flowers average seven inches across. To make this print, I used the following materials:

- Water-based block printing inks (such as Graphic Chemical brand)
- Water-soluble vehicle (such as Graphic Chemical brand)
- 3-inch brayer
- 1-inch brayer
- Watercolor paints
- Watercolor brushes
- Watercolor palette
- Container of water
- One 22-inch by 30-inch sheet of Evanescent paper
- Newsprint
- Tweezers
- Ink spreaders
- Glass palette
- Flowering hibiscus plants
- Telephone directory and heavy book (for pressing iris)

Pressing

The hisbiscus plant requires no pressing at all since the leaves are flat. To keep them for winter use, put them in a press. When you remove the leaves from the press, moisten them slightly between sheets of damp newspaper. The flowers can only be printed fresh.

Because the flower petals have a slight curve, pressing usually creates wrinkles. I simply cut several long stems of the hibiscus and other flowering plants I plan to print and put them in vases of water so I can prepare each petal, leaf, and stem as I am about to ink and print it. Also, I like to be able to refer to the natural form of the plant in the vases to compose the picture as I go along.

Printing the Flower

The flowers are the focus of this print and dictate the placement of the leaves and stems so the flowers should be printed first. I began my print by removing the six ray petals of the hibiscus one by one, and inking and printing each in turn. Using both light and dark colors adds variation and achieves a sense of dimension.

I trimmed some of the petals at the point where they joined to create the curved appearance they have when the blossom is whole. The wide petals were inked with several passes from a 1-inch brayer, covering a portion of the petal each time to avoid wrinkling, and was then printed by hand pressing. The petals disintegrate after just one print and cannot be used again.

The pistil must be flattened before being inked and printed. Instead of actually printing it, I usually draw it in with a pencil and paint it later with watercolor. The stem is handled in this way, as well. To appear natural, the entire stem shouldn't be visible.

Printing the Leaves

The hibiscus leaves can be printed in the "walking" press, laid out in a natural formation overlapping and cascading across the paper. They should look like they're

Hibiscus and Iris. *The hibiscus flower is simply inked and printed, with no pressing, while the iris must be dissected and pressed first. For best results, pick flowers on the same day they are to be printed.*

generating from the stem. I added a very light "stem" pencil line (later erased) to guide leaf placement.

I don't use the same leaf twice in one print because nature doesn't make the same leaf twice! To make the most of my time and materials, I usually work on several pictures at the same time, so I can use the hibiscus leaves as part of other compositions as well. These sturdy, interesting leaves stand up to many printings.

Iris

The complex iris flower should be pressed before printing for best results. See page 13 for instructions.

To print the iris shown on the previous page, I pressed the flowers for twenty minutes, then gently inked the flattened, but still firm, flowers with a brayer and dabbers. To print, I laid each flower inked-side down on the printmaking paper and pressed with my hand. As with the hibiscus, the iris flowers should be printed before the leaves and, for a consistent appearance to the composition, the stems were penciled in and painted with watercolors. To enhance the color of the flowers, I applied a watercolor wash of cobalt violet to the dry print.

PRINTING FRUITS, VEGETABLES, & OTHER NATURAL OBJECTS

The same materials and techniques described in Chapters 3 and 4 for basic nature printing are applied to printing other natural objects, with allowances made to accommodate different forms. For a materials list, see *Basic Direct Printing* or *Watercolor Printing* in Chapter 4.

Fruits and Vegetables

Leafy vegetables or leafy vegetable tops (such as those from carrots and radishes) can be inked and printed the same way as any other leaf (see page 33). Before beginning, assemble the following materials:

- Watercolor paints or water-based inks
- Watercolor brushes or artist's bristle brushes and/or dabbers
- Newsprint

Before it was printed, this partially eaten apple was cut in half and painted with watercolors. After printing, the seeds were penciled in and colored with a brush.

- Printmaking paper
- Tweezers (for leafy vegetables)
- Watercolor palette or glass palette (for inks)
- Paper towels
- Soap (for clean-up)

Preparation for Printing

To print the fruit or vegetable body, first cut it in half or in thick slices to create flat surfaces. Cutting the fruit in half reveals seeds and other inner structures, which produce interesting printed images. Fruits and vegetables tend to have a high moisture content. Blot the cut

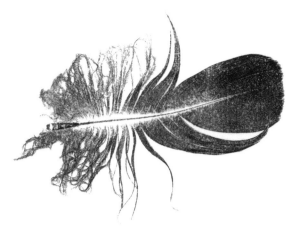

Goosefeather print.

Scallop shell print.

surfaces well with absorbent cloth or paper towels for several minutes to absorb as much moisture as possible before painting or inking.

Inking and Printing

Since moisture repels ink, watercolors are often preferable to inks for printing fruits and vegetables. You can also use water-based inks that are made to mix with water instead of vehicle. To apply pigment, dab or brush the watercolor paint or ink onto the halved fruit or vegetable. Place the halved fruit paint-side down on the printing surface. Press well using hand pressure and remove carefully.

Seashells and Shelled Animals

Shells found on the beach or shellfish (flat shells such as clam and scallop are the easiest to print) can be nature printed once they have been cleaned and dried thoroughly. Shells print well on fabric, as well as on paper, and since they don't deteriorate as plants do, they can be printed countless times.

You will need the following materials for printing seashells:

- Ink
- Artist's bristle brushes
- Sumi paper, other soft Asian paper, or fabric
- Plastic modeling clay
- Water
- Paper towels
- Appropriate clean up supplies

Inking

Using plastic modeling clay, form a pedestal that is slightly smaller in width than the shell, and push the shell into the clay. This will hold the shell in place for inking and printing. Ink the shell with bristle brushes, until it is evenly coated.

Secure the shell on a clay base for inking.

Printing

Lay printing paper or fabric over the shell and rub with fingers to transfer the ink. Another method is to allow the ink to dry on the shell, dampen a soft paper (thicker than sumi) with a damp blotter, and press it gently against the shell. The damp paper will moisten and lift the ink.

Gyotaku/"Fish Rubbing"

Developed in Japan in the early nineteenth century as a method for sportsmen to preserve caught game fish, *gyotaku* has come to be practiced as an art form. Before printing, assemble the following materials:

- Powdered cleanser or vinegar
- Water
- Paper towels
- Water-based ink
- Flat artist's bristle brushes (½-inch to 1-inch, depending on the size of the fish you will be printing)
- Soft artist's brush (small and round) for painting the eye
- Newspapers
- Newsprint paper
- Sumi printing paper
- Plastic modeling clay
- Straight pins
- A very fresh fish*

*Flat fish are easier to work with, and those with pronounced scales produce more textured prints. Keep fish cold until you are ready to work. If frozen, thaw before inking. If you don't like the smell, buy a paper mask from the hardware store and rub the outside of it with fresh herbs or a dab of perfume or essential oil.

Preparation for Printing

Clean the outside of the fish with cleanser or vinegar and water, rinse thoroughly, and dry well. Plug the mouth, anus, and gills with paper to keep moisture from leaking out. Remove the eye, or leave it uninked, as it doesn't print well.

Place the fish on a flat surface padded with newspapers. Use plastic modeling clay to keep the spread fins in position and to hold the fish in place. If necessary, stick pins through the fins and into clay to hold securely.

Inking

Using a bristle brush, spread ink thinly across the fish from head to tail. Repeat in the opposite direction from tail to head for further definition of the scales.

Gyotaku print: *Carp* by Shingo Takahashi of Japan, combines nature printing techniques for fish, plants, flowers, insects and rocks.

Spread ink thinly across the fish with a bristle brush, working from head to tail. Leave the eye uninked since it doesn't print well.

Printing

Since the first print made often contains some excess moisture and mucus, I recommend using newsprint for this "trial" print. Lay the sheet of newsprint over the inked fish and rub firmly with one hand while holding the paper in place with the other hand. Press with your fingers to impress the features of the head area, then do the same along the body all the way to the tail. Carefully remove the printed sheet of paper. Reink your fish and use sumi or another soft Japanese or Chinese paper to make additional prints in the same manner. A fresh fish will yield eight to ten prints.

To finish, paint in the fish's eye using a small, round soft brush. Paint a black pupil with an off-center unpainted white spot to represent reflected light. Surround the pupil with a colored wash to represent the iris.

Taku-ga

Nanjo Kubota, an artist in Japan, creates *Taku-ga,* which means "rubbing picture," as shown. *Taku-ga,* a registered trademark, is a technique created by Nanjo's father, Katsuhiko Miyaji, which is displayed as a traditional hanging scroll. The "rubbing picture" is made by spraying plants with a sumi ink solution and then printing directly from the plants. The print is then colored with watercolors.

To practice Taku-ga, you will need the following materials:

- One plywood sheet and two polyurethane foam boards (both larger than the plant being printed)

- Black sumi ink, diluted with water and a drop of mild detergent

- Hand stroking "flit" pump sprayer, or bug spray gun (available at hardware stores) filled with the sumi ink mixture

- Tweezers, one or two pairs

Taku-ga print of chrysanthemums by Nanjo Kubota of Japan.

- Rolling pin or dowel
- Printmaking paper, such as Washi or other kozo fiber
- Watercolor paints and brushes
- Water
- Palette for mixing watercolors
- Pressed plants
- Newsprint paper
- Newspapers

Preparation for Printing

Arrange a sheet of polyurethane foam on top of a sheet of plywood; cover with a sheet of newsprint. Lay pressed plant on a sheet of newspaper. Spray a light mist of sumi ink mixture onto the plant with the spray gun. Using the tweezers, move the sprayed plant to the waiting sheet of newsprint, inked-side up, arranging your composition. The proportion of a taku-ga print should be approximately seven parts object to three parts space, and, ideally, the space should be balanced around the main flower.

Printing

Position the printmaking sheet over the plant and top with another sheet of polyurethane foam. Roll the rolling pin or dowel over the foam sheet, applying pressure to transfer the image.

For taku-ga, sumi ink is applied with a spray gun.

Coloring Finished Print

After the sumi image dries, color the nature print with swift brush strokes of watercolor washes. Do not paint twice in the same spot. A rhythm of dark and light is important. Make the most of the black color of sumi ink to express its elegant beauty. To make it an authentic taku-ga print, you should apply your personal seal (stamp of the artist's signature), positioned to enhance the composition. When completely dry, mount the translucent paper onto sturdy paper or board with very thin rice or wheat paste.

Spider Webs

The perfect design of a common garden spider's orb web, glittering with dew in the early morning sun, is beautiful to behold.

Just as we don't disturb the roots when cutting precious flowers so that the flowers will return, we don't want to kill the spider in the process of making a web print. Nature printer Gudrun Garkisch is careful to first shoo away the spider so she is not harmed — within an hour, the spider will build another web. With Ms. Garkisch's technique, you can produce two prints at once from one web. You will need an assistant for this printing process, along with the following materials:

- Two sheets of 4-ply matboard, foam board, or other stiff board (larger than the spider web you will be printing) and strong paper strips for handles.
- Roll of strong tape
- Two sheets of soft white printing paper such as Hosho, the same size as the matboard or foam board
- Large metal bulldog or binder clips or tape
- Large ruler
- Paper or fabric shield (for containing the spray paint to immediate area)

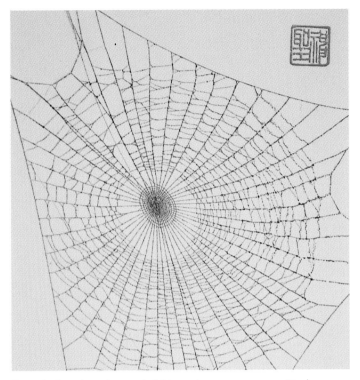

Detail of spiderweb, entitled Neat, *by nature printer Gudrun Garkisch, 11 inches by 14 inches.*

- Can of spray paint (preferably black, oil-based Rustoleum brand)
- Spray fixative for artwork

Preparation for Printing

Measure the spider web and cut the two sheets of board and the printing paper to exceed the dimensions of the web. Create a handle for the back of each board by cutting two strips of paper, each approximately 8 inches long. Affix one strip to the middle of the back of each board with strong tape. Secure the printing paper to the right side of each board with the clips or tape.

Printing

Take your prepared boards, spray paint, and paper or fabric shield outdoors to the site of the web. Shield the area around the web (you may need someone to assist you in holding this). If the spider is present, shoo her away. Carefully spray the web lightly on both sides. All the threads must remain intact, especially the web's supporting threads.

Slip your hands through the makeshift handles on the boards. Wasting no time (since the paint dries quickly), gently bring one board to the web so that it comes evenly in contact with the paper. Holding the first board steady, bring the second board up against the other side of the web until it meets the first board. Have your assistant firmly hold the boards together while you slip your hands out of the holders and press or rub the outsides of the boards to transfer the image. Separate the boards, remove the sheets of paper, and let the prints dry. Spray with fixative.

NATURE PRINTING WITHOUT INK OR PAINT

There are a few natural objects and some printing papers that make it possible to obtain a nature print without applying any pigment to the natural object. Following are two techniques I've experimented with that you may enjoy as well.

Mushroom Spores

Superstitions and stories abound about the fungi we call mushrooms, which spring up with amazing rapidity in warm, moist places. Long associated with fairies, elves, and witches, some delicious mushrooms are edible, but some are deadly. The part of the mushroom growing aboveground is the fruiting body, and the growing mass of dense white mycelium underneath the ground is the vegetative part.

Containing no chlorophyll, mushrooms are never green, but they may be white, red, yellow, lavender, silvery blue, pink, or orange, and exhibit a variety of shapes. The common field mushroom is white with pinkish-brown gills, with platelike growths radiating underneath the cap. Spores develop on each side of the gills. Very small one-celled organisms, spores are like the seeds of flowering plants that scatter with the wind and develop into new mycelium, sometimes living for centuries.

To print mushrooms, you will need the following materials:

- Mushrooms

- Light- and dark-colored papers

- Cups or glasses

- Artists' spray fixative

Preparation for Printing

Cut the stem off at the cap of a mushroom and lay the cap on a sheet of paper with the gills facing the paper. For dark spores, use white paper; for light spores, use black paper. If you are unsure of the color, make prints on both light- and dark-colored paper.

Printing

Place an inverted cup or glass over the mushroom cap and leave it undisturbed for twelve to twenty-four hours. Remove the glass and the cap to reveal the pattern of spores that have shed along the lines of the radiating gills. To keep the print intact, spray with one or two coatings of pastel or charcoal artists' fixative.

Cyanotype

An early photographic process, cyanotype is simply a blueprint. The process uses paper that has been treated with blue dye which undergoes a chemical reaction after being exposed to the sun and then immersed in plain water. Objects laid on top of the paper are silhouetted by sunlight. To print, assemble the following materials:

- Cyanotype or Nature Printing paper*

- One plywood sheet and one glass sheet of the same size (slightly larger than your paper)

- Felt cut to cover plywood sheet

- Bulldog or spring clips, or weights

- Pan of water

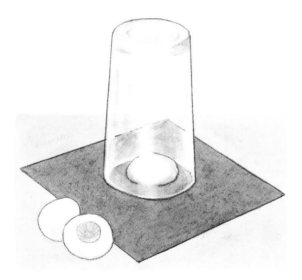

Mushroom spore prints appear after 12 to 24 hours.

Cyanotype of iris resulting from a chemical reaction to the sun.

- Warm iron
- A sunny day

* This is a product name. See Appendix for ordering information.

Preparation for Printing

Nature printer John Doughty, who has made many cyanotype nature prints suggests using pressed lacy plants such as yarrow, Queen Anne's lace, artemesia, and baby's breath. The veining of delicate, translucent leaves and flowers appears prominently when the flower pigment and the leaf chlorophyll have been first eliminated. To do this, press plant until dry, then expose to sunlight until color disappears, a process that could take months. Opaque areas of the plant will appear in silhouette on the print.

Printing

Follow the directions for cyanotype paper on the package. To begin, cover the plywood with the felt. Arrange plants of the same thickness on blue side of cyanotype paper, place on felt, and cover with sheet of glass. Secure the glass and plywood together with clips or weights. Lay it flat, glass-side up in the full sun for three to thirty minutes, depending on the type of plants, time of day, and season. The stronger the sun, the less time needed.

Take the clipped unit back inside and remove clips, glass, and plants. Dip exposed paper into a cool bath of plain water for one minute. Lay the paper flat and, when dry, press smooth with a warm iron.

Lay the prepared cyanotype in the sun for 3 to 30 minutes.

Printing the Human Body

As we think of printing living things and natural objects, the human body is fair game. Prints of body parts have both practical and artistic uses. Footprints and fingerprints are used for keeping records and identifying babies and lawbreakers. Dentists make casts of their patients' teeth. I've heard of a Hollywood make-up man who has collected prints from famous lips and an artist in New York with a print collection of ordinary lips.

There are also artists who practice whole body printing — quite an intricate feat. To do this by a direct printing process, you apply nontoxic pigment to cover the skin on the side of the body that will be printed and then lean the body against a large sheet of vertically supported paper.

There is also an indirect process for printing the whole body, as achieved by artist Volker Busmann of Frankfurt, Germany. Busmann has his human subject back into a door-sized frame covered with a flexible film of latex. A breathing tube is essential, as the next step is to spray the front of the subject with another film of latex. Moments later, after the sprayed layer has dried, the air is vacuumed out, creating a perfect casting which is then sprayed with pigment while the person insides continues to breath through the tube. Mr. Busmann then makes his print by pressing paper over the inked subject. He has also printed fleshy plants and inanimate objects such as musical instruments with his technique, which is internationally copyrighted.

CHAPTER 6

PRACTICING THE ART OF NATURE PRINTING

—🍃—

There are four **components** to learning how to successfully practice nature printing as an art form: Acquiring the practical skills for using the necessary materials and techniques; becoming aware of the creative resources within you; seeing with the eye of an artist; and acquiring knowledge of your subject, especially visual knowledge. These skills and knowledge are critical to any visual art. By carefully reading and practicing the steps described in Chapters 2 through 5, you will master the first component of this process — acquiring the practical skills of nature printing. The other three components may seem a bit more elusive. But they're not as difficult as you might think.

The wife rules when sage grows vig... the garden.

...

He that would live for aye, must ea...

An exceedingly pleasant scent, one I always favor.

A sage leaf, nature printed by Leonardo da Vinci c. 1500, continues to be one of my favorite plants to print.

flower language -esteem-

Sage

Salvia officinalis

THE CREATIVE SPARK

Nature's simplicity is so powerful and yet so subtle that it often escapes our notice. When you do make a connection with nature's power and simplicity, such as when you're suddenly awestruck by the scent of a spring day, or the crystal pattern on a frosty window pane, it is not your conscious mind at work but your "innermost awareness, awakeness, and knowledge," as poet Rainer Maria Rilke observed.

Everyone engages in creative thinking — whether you are at home trying to organize the household, at work deciphering genetic codes, or in the garden composing nature-printed pictures. As you learn to nature print, it is important to recognize that solving any creative challenge is a process involving several stages. In nature printing, the first stage is to learn as much as possible about nature itself.

LEARNING ABOUT DESIGN IN NATURE

The simple act of nature printing can open a deeper realization for those practicing this art. While recreating images of our natural world, the beauty before us becomes our own. We want to know more about the splendid subjects of nature, which are at once ethereal and replete. Being spirited by the sight of drifting, colorful autumn leaves or the view of a wildflower field moves creative energies. But to illustrate thoughtful depictions of nature up close, we need to acquire a deeper visual knowledge of the natural world around us. The best way to improve nature-printed compositions is to know your subjects well.

Trust in Nature, in what is simple in Nature, in the small Things that hardly anyone sees and that can so suddenly become huge, immeasurable; ... then everything will become easier for you, more coherent and somehow more reconciling, not in your conscious mind perhaps, which stays behind, astonished, but in your innermost awareness, awakeness, and knowledge.
— Rainer Maria Rilke

Hone Your Observational Skills

Examine an individual plant. Is it small and delicate, strong and firm, or somewhere in-between? Is the color grayed or vibrant? Feel the texture. Is it smooth and glossy, soft and downy, pebbled or ribbed? Use your field guide glossary to determine botanical terms for plant structures. Is the stem round, square, or flat? Are the leaves entire, toothed, or lobed? Are they opposite, alternate, or whorled on the stem? Do the veins protrude?

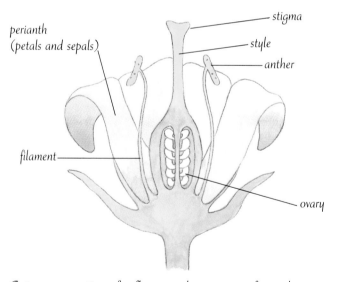

Cut a cross section of a flower and use a magnifying glass to appreciate the details of its parts.

Good observational skills are basic to nature printing. For example: observe that sage leaves (left) are downy and pebbled; mint (center) has a square stem and opposite leaves; and the double-winged fruit of maple trees (right) contains the seed.

Observe the plant as it unfurls. Look for sepals, stipules, tendrils, leaf buds, fiddleheads, or spores. Remove it from the soil to see the tubers, roots, rhizomes, or runners. Using a magnifying glass, examine the many parts of a flower and cut a vertical cross section of a flower bud with a sharp razor blade to view the inside. Remember to take notice throughout the seasons of all stages of plant development.

Nature printing shows the beauty of nature's patterns. The seemingly infinite variety of patterns and shapes in nature becomes clearly finite when reading *Patterns in Nature,* by Peter S. Stevens. Some of the recurring natural patterns that Stevens describes are branching, spiraling, meandering, explosion, turbulence, contour, and stress. As an architect, Stevens emphasizes the mathematical predictability of nature. As an artist, I find the patterns of nature aesthetically fascinating.

The branching pattern, for example, is seen in leaf veining, butterfly wing markings, root systems, water channeling, ice crystals, and blood vessels. Explosions take place in stars and volcanoes and can be seen in the streaming rays of the sun; yet the explosion pattern also occurs in the diminutive daisy. From the center disc of this sim-

ple flower bursts its radiating petals. As if mimicking the sun, the name daisy comes from its old English name, "day's eye." The globe thistle is another floral example of the explosion pattern in nature. Linear explosions can be seen in lightning bolts and the flowering spike of the foxtail lily.

Turbulence, the primordial pattern, is found in the whirls of moving water and clouds. The spiral pattern occurs in the unfurling tendrils of grape, morning glory, and other vines, and in fiddlehead ferns, honeysuckle stems, ranunculus flower petals, and sunflower seed heads; also finger prints, the muscles of the apex of the human heart, countless shells of sea animals, bones, horns, antlers, spider webs, and tornadoes. Microscopic organisms such as bacteria and protozoa exhibit all of these natural patterns. In *The Curves of Life,* by Theodore Andrea Cook, we learn that the spiral formation was widely used as a decorative pattern throughout the

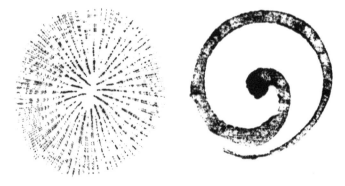

The explosion pattern (left) and the spiral pattern (right) are revealed in these prints of seashells.

ancient world as a symbol for "creative power or energy, the strength and divinity of the sun … and many sacred phenomena of life." The genes which produce who we are, the DNA double helix, is a molecular spiral; and the galaxy we live in, the Milky Way, is a cosmological spiral. The universe itself is an enormous turbulence.

By design, all of nature consists of the same patterns and particles of matter that constitute life. Categorizing the patterns of nature brings a visual connection to seemingly different things, making us realize that differences have existed only insofar as we have been unable to recognize what is, in fact, fundamentally similar.

Increase Your Knowledge about Plants

I find that my memory for conceptual, sensing, and visual information is stronger than my memory for facts. I often need to refer to my notes and books to recall facts. If you have a similar problem, you realize that knowing where to find information when you need it is almost as good as having many facts memorized. Field guides such as those by The Audubon Society, Roger Tory Peterson, and Lawrence Newcomb are essential for the nature printer. Your local library and the Inter-Library Loan (ILL) program are unlimited resources for information.

Learn the common and scientific names of the plants you work with and become familiar with the functions of their parts and the appearance of their structure. This knowledge will deepen your appreciation and help you create more accurate, detailed nature-printed compositions. Admire the plants you nature print, taking some time to carefully look at and learn about them.

For hands-on investigating, begin in your own backyard. Learn as much as you can about the plants growing there, beginning with the most common. Find a nice juicy dandelion, scientifically known as

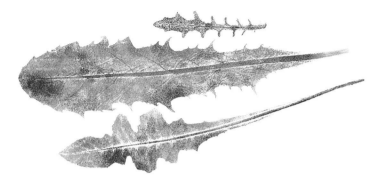

Dandelion. *The divided, sometimes pubescent, leaves of this readily available, unappreciated wild plant have many lobes, ranging from shallow to deep-cut, that provide interesting shape and texture for nature printing.*

Taraxacum officinale. Dandelions propagate by sending a globe of parachuting seeds away on the breezes or on the breath of a child who picks one. The divided, sometimes pubescent, leaves of this readily available, unappreciated wild plant have many shallow to deep-cut lobes that provide an interesting shape and texture for nature printing.

DESIGNING PRINTS

To create gardens, gardeners work with many of the same elements that artists work with to create pictures — color, space, light, form, focal point, and others. While these elements are applied differently to planning a garden than they are to designing garden art, there is a connection. As a garden artist, I have two basic design schemes for my nature prints. I call them *the cottage garden* and *the formal garden*.

A cottage garden, as shown, evokes feelings of activity, happy meandering, and busyness. This is a natural plan that allows vines to seek and climb, and combines close plantings of low-growing, part-shade plants crowded in between taller, sun-loving blooms. This design doesn't require a focal point. In fact, the lack of focus on any one plant or grouping adds to the sense of vigorous wandering.

In contrast, the formal garden always has a focal point, as shown on page 62. A fountain, sundial, sculpture, or large central planting can provide that point from which all other components of the garden extend. Symmetry, not meandering, is imperative. Planning ahead is more important to a formal garden than the plan-as-you-go attitude of a cottage garden. Orderly rows of vegetables, trimmed borders, neat paths, and plants carefully arranged according to color, height, and sea-

Every garden-maker should be an artist along his own lines . . . . The tiniest garden is often the loveliest."

— Vita Sackville-West

son are all hallmarks of the serene, controlled atmosphere of the formal garden.

One advantage in designing nature-printed compositions is the ease of working with the actual pressed plants that will be used to create the picture. Unlike other visual arts, preliminary sketches are not necessary in

The Cottage Garden design evokes feelings of happy meandering and busyness.

ARTEMISIA-RUE-GERANIUM-RED CLOVER-Queen Anne's LACe-LAVender

The *Formal Garden* design depicts a serene, controlled atmosphere.

nature printing. Simply choose the pressed plants you wish to use and arrange and rearrange them on the paper until you are satisfied with your composition. Then make a few marks in light pencil to indicate placement of the plants before removing them for remoisturizing if necessary and inking.

Basic Design Elements

As a beginning nature print, it is helpful to make smaller prints with just a few images first, and then progress into larger, more complicated designs where some elements will dominate over others. There are some basic aspects of design that can help you in this process of arranging your plants. Consider each of the following factors in turn and its relationship to the others as they combine to form a pleasing composition. I refer to printing plants on paper for the sake of convenience, but this design information applies to all types of nature printing. In fact, the basic elements of design briefly described here are applicable to all visual art media.

Size

The size of your print may be predetermined by the amount of space available on the wall you wish to decorate, by a frame or piece of fabric you want to use, or some similar physical condition. Sometimes, the number and size of the items you plan to print determines the finished size. To determine the size required, lay out the pressed plants on a large sheet of paper and arrange and rearrange the plants while considering your design. When you come to an agreeable composition, measure the horizontal and vertical dimensions of your design and add a few more inches to procure a generous margin as needed for matting.

The Power of Negative Space

For centuries, artists in Asia have especially valued the visual impact of negative space and used it expertly, often as a dominant aspect of their pictures. One example is in the nature printing technique taku-ga (see page 51). The creator of this technique consciously designates the proportions of three parts space to seven parts object for all prints.

The margin around the edges of a matted picture confines the positive as well as negative space. The inner border of the mat "traps" the negative space within the picture plane. If the margin is too narrow, the design will appear cramped. If it is too wide, the picture will appear lost and floating. To determine the desired space within the matted margins of your picture as you are compos-ing it or before matting it, try laying four long strips of matboard (at least three inches wide) to create the edges of your picture plane. Move the margin strips, changing the width and length of the picture space, to determine where you want the edges of the composition.

Focal Point

Most compositions need a focal point around which the rest of the design can be created. Most of my formal garden designs have a focal point. The focal point should be centrally located in the picture, not close to an edge or corner, and it is always the most important element of the design. The rhythm and movement of the composition, which is created by the lines and spaces in the images of your design, should both stem from and lead to the focal point, thereby achieving unity of composition.

Space

The space within a picture is either positive or negative. Positive space is space that is filled with the image. Negative space contains no image, but this space is not empty, i.e., it is not inactive or incidental to the total picture. The positioning of positive and negative space is as important to design as the image itself. Shapes resulting from configurations of positive and negative space contribute to the underlying rhythm of composition. In short, keep in mind that what you don't print can contribute as much to your design as what you do print.

Line

Alphabets are nothing more than a series of lines that were originated eons ago. And writing — just like painting, nature printing, or any visual art — is a symbolic visual language to be read and interpreted by the viewer. Your signature is an expression of you, just as the veins of a leaf or the wrinkles of time on a human face are lines expressive of the character of that leaf or that face. In most of my work, line is a key design element used to express the nature of the depicted objects and define the space within a composition.

In plant prints, expressive line is formed by the edges and veining of leaves and flowers, and by roots, stems, tendrils, and other elongated parts. Disconnected lines will visually connect when one ends and another begins in close proximity. Pay attention to compositional direction created by the angles of dominant lines.

All design elements act as visual interpretations of intangible ideas. For example, lines that curve, swirl, or intersect create movement and interest, but they can also create chaos. Unless chaos is the theme of your design, remember, less is more.

Tone

Think of the tones of your picture on an imagined scale of white (lightest) to black (darkest). When mixing colors, keep in mind their place on the continuum, according to how light or dark each color appears to be. If an individual leaf or flower contains light, medium, and dark tones, the light areas may appear to be reflect-ing light, while darker areas seem to be in shadow. The use of light, medium, and dark tones is also useful in creating dimension.

Tone contributes to the mood of a composition. High contrast is created when using mostly lights and darks with few or no medium tones. For example, a stark white background displaying dark, bold prints feels vibrant or intense. When medium tones dominate the picture, such as a soft colored background with medium-toned prints, the mood is calmer, more gentle.

Dimension

One way to give the illusion of three dimensions in your prints is to combine light, medium, and dark tones. The lights will appear to be in the background, the dark or brightest tones will appear to be in the foreground, with the medium tones somewhere in between. By making smaller specimens light toned and larger specimens dark, you achieve a further illusion of dimension. We strive to create clear, crisp nature prints, but for added distance you may intentionally shift and blur some of the light-toned prints, making them appear even farther in the background. This must be done with care, however, because if too pronounced, the blurred prints can look in error. A focal point should be sharp and primarily bright or dark toned as part of the foreground or as an integral design element.

Composition

Large and small shapes should be positioned with equal weight. If one section of the picture looks too "heavy," the balance of the whole is disrupted. Color and space also have weight. These qualities can be considered by imagining light and dark areas for your composition as the plants are being

Waterlilies and Cranberries, 22 inches by 30 inches. The chaotic intertwining of waterlilies and cranberry vines is the theme for this watercolor nature print painting.

arranged and by viewing the spaces as an integral part of the design.

If your composition includes a focal point, place this first with the other components surrounding it. If there is no focal point place the most important, or largest, components of the picture first. Themes, such as "spring flowers" or "greens of winter," dictate the feeling you want your composition to project.

The best way to learn how to compose a picture is to consciously observe artwork in books, museums, libraries, and other public buildings. Visit the art galleries in your area and look at the shapes, forms and colors of the pictures. Ask yourself why some of the pictures appeal to you but others don't. Try to see what is harmonious, gentle, and tranquil as opposed to what appears forceful or in turmoil. Good composition requires careful consideration of all the design elements within the context of your theme or idea.

COLOR

Pigments of the earth as well as dyes made from plants, animals, and insects provided color for prehistoric civilizations to adorn their skin, clothing, implements, and homes. The earth's natural ores and minerals continue to serve artists as sources of color. Since the recent development of more durable and lightfast synthetics, the colors derived from plants, animals, and insects are rarely used in commercial production of artists' materials.

Visual artists work with color every day. Attempts to capture the essence of a delicate violet primrose or the strength of a brilliant yellow sunflower, and experiments with mixing and layering pigments in pursuit of defining a certain emotion or attitude, are the challenges of color. There are countless books devoted to this captivating subject. See the Appendix after having read the basic information in this chapter.

The Language of Flowers

The Victorian practice of flower language, popular during the nineteenth century, has made a modest revival. Floral dictionaries of the time listed the names of flowers, herbs, and other plants followed by their symbolic meanings. For example, roses symbolize beauty and love, violets represent modesty, and pansies mean "think of me." The language of color plays a role within the language of flowers. Red roses signify love and desire; yellow roses are for friendship; pink roses represent grace and gentleness, and so on. A carefully chosen bouquet of flowers and plants in certain colors conveys a very specific message. If you fancy the Language of Flowers, why not create nature-printed images that convey a specific message. Print the plants that correspond to the words and feelings you want to express. You can label the plants and denote their language, or write a note on the meaning of the nature print and send it to someone you adore.

Color Terms and Color in the Garden

Primary colors. These are red, yellow, and blue. They cannot be produced by mixing.

Secondary colors. These colors are produced by mixing two primary colors. Red and yellow make orange, blue and red make purple, and yellow and blue make green.

Tertiary colors. These shades of various browns, maroons, grays, and blacks are produced by the mixing the three primary colors or two secondary colors.

Alstromeria in the Sky, watercolor nature print, 14¾ inches by 22¼ inches.

Complementary colors. The complement of a primary color is the mixture of the other two primaries. When you mix the primaries red and yellow to make orange, the third primary is blue. Therefore, blue is the complement of orange. Red and blue make purple, with yellow being its complement. Blue and yellow make green, so red is the complement of green.

The striking quality of red immediately draws our attention but seems particularly vibrant in the garden. A red rose or poppy, surrounded by the complement of green leaves, seems to vibrate. Complementary colors are important in picture making because they set off one another to best advantage, just as they do in nature. Use complementary colors side by side for resonant results.

Conversely, mixing complementary pigments will soften them. For example, a touch of green added to red will tone down the red. Rather than adding gray or black pigment, which can deaden the color, a bit of a color's complement will subdue and deepen the color. And a near equal mixture of two complements creates interesting grays and blacks with colorful undertones.

Warm and cool colors. Some colors emit warmth, while others appear cool. This is partly a personal, emotional response to a particular color and, as a color effect, is dependent on the other colors surrounding it. Warm colors are active and advancing, while cool colors are passive and retreating. Generally, the warm colors are red, orange, and yellow; cool colors are blue, purple, and violet. Green is both cool and warm, an ambivalent color.

Reflected color is the color of something reflecting off something else. Some reflected color is readily apparent, as blue sky and bright sun seen in the calm surface of a puddle. Sky and sunshine also reflect off glossy periwinkle leaves and waxy lilies. Be sure to look for less obvious flickerings, such as a purple eggplant reflecting off the edge of a neighboring flower petal or the green glow cast onto a pale concrete birdbath from encircling foliage.

Especially in simple nature print compositions, I like to exaggerate the use of reflected color to visually communicate activity, such as a breeze and the buzz of bees or the feeling of the sun's warmth. Reflected color combined with local color makes for interesting images.

Local color. This is simply the intrinsic color of something. A daffodil is yellow, and its leaves are green. However, nature is much more subtle than this and shouldn't be observed with such matter-of-factness.

Color in Light and Shade. Color and light are essentially the same thing. Colors appear brightest in bright light. In shade, colors recede, losing some of their brilliance. Cast shadows appear cool in color. Observe light and color during the mist of early morning, the clouds or sunshine of afternoon, and the haze of evening. Time of day, and the direction and quality of light creates differing moods. Note the characteristics of light as intense, filtered, or shadowed.

In the dark of evening, red is the first color to recede. White and yellow reflect light best and remain visible the longest. Blossoms of these colors, and the silvery foliage of lamb's ears, mullein pinks, certain artemesias, and other plants of this character, seem to glow in moonlight, lending themselves well as border plants to light the path for an evening stroll. Become sensitive to light and color, and experiment with translating these sensations in your nature prints.

(Left) Everlasting Pea and Red Clover, 15 inches by 22 inches. (Right) Detail, Lily Pads, 22 inches by 30 inches.

DISPLAYING PRINTS

A red rose in the garden, surrounded by its complement of green leaves, seems to vibrate.

For the best protection and enhancement of nature prints on paper, mat and frame them under glass or plastic. Choose mat colors and frame mouldings to complement the nature prints. A frame contains the art, separating it from the surroundings. A mat creates visual space around the art for viewing and air space between the art and the glass, allowing air circulation which greatly reduces the possibility of bacterial growth.

Consult a professional framer, visit a do-it-yourself frame shop, or purchase foam board backing sheets, ready-made frames and hardware, and pre-cut mats available in standard sizes from art and craft suppliers. When matting and framing nature prints that have been produced on archival or acid free papers, be sure to mat and back them with museum quality or, at least, acid free materials to extend the life of the art. These materials are more costly, but provide proper protection for valued artwork.

An Appreciation of the Subtleties of Color in Nature

Louise Beebe Wilder's extensive knowledge of flowers and careful observation of color are apparent as she describes a "white garden" in **What Happens in My Garden**, published in 1935. "Now it would be natural to suppose that a garden planted wholly with white flowers would be bleak in effect, or at least very monotonous; but this was not at all the case…. It was frank and fresh and full of changing values…. A large proportion of so-called white flowers tend towards buff, or mauve or blush in the throat; the petals of many are delicately lined, or veined or blotched with color — blue, carmine, green, yellow. A great number are not white at all but what we call cream-white, blush-white or skimmed-milk white, and the name of those having a greenish cast is legion. Many flowers change from white to pink or even to deep rose or yellow as they age, while bunches of bright-hued stamens or stigmata often cast a glow over the whole flower. Things being as they are, there could not possibly be monotony of tone in a garden of white flowers."

Two methods of mounting nature prints: At left, leaves decoupaged onto a black frame add further ornament to a simple watercolor nature print; at right, a nature print on fabric or paper such as sumi fastened to an inexpensive wooden embroidery hoop makes interesting wall art or an unusual gift.

Alternative Display Ideas and Tips

- Crop nature prints so that the margin is even all around, slip prints into sturdy clear plastic envelopes (from art store or office supplier), and tack them onto a wall or wall-mounted cork strips.

- Mount a length of moulding to a wall, with lip facing up, and line up a collection of firmly backed and/or matted prints.

- Plate stands or small table easels make appropriate holders for matted prints and for nature printed herbals or journals.

- Rotate all of your nature print collections regularly to keep dust and light from deteriorating prints that are unprotected by glass or plastic.

- Store unprotected prints in mylar or acid free paper envelopes in a cool, dark, airy place.

- Acrylic box frames are inexpensive and come in a large variety of sizes, and it is very easy to insert and remove prints so they can be changed frequently. Make a wall arrangement with several box frames to be changed seasonally, for holidays, or just to accommodate your latest nature prints.

- Nature prints on fabric, or even soft Asian papers such as sumi, can be fastened on very inexpensive wooden embroidery hoops for interesting wall art or a pleasing gift. Use fabric markers for lettering or a border on both fabric and paper (regular markers bleed on soft papers).

Mounting Prints

Mounting removes wrinkles resulting from pressing paper into crevices of fish, shells, and other objects when printing, and creates a firm base for prints made on soft, lightweight Asian papers. Artists' spray adhesives are an easy solution for small nature prints. Spray the back of the print and attach it to heavy paper or board (follow label directions). Don't use this method for artwork you value, as spray adhesive products are not permanent and, in time, will discolor the paper. Dry mounting with inert adhesives applied with heat can be a viable alternative. Consult a reliable, professional frame shop for this service.

Wet mounting with wheat or rice paste is the traditional method. The wet mounting process can be reversed with water, and the artwork removed from the backing.

For more information, I highly recommend the book *Matting, Mounting, and Framing Art,* by Max Hyder (see Appendix).

NATURE PRINTING PROJECTS

I continue to be amazed by the inventive applications nature printers use to create decorative, practical items. The most unusual use that I've seen was a nature-printed jeep. Some of the leaf images were direct prints, but most were silhouettes. It looked like leaves had been secured to the jeep's surface, which was then spray painted. After the leaves were removed and the paint dried, a second and third layer of leaves and paint had been applied. Direct leaf prints had been added last. The result was very attractive, done in beige, light green, and tan.

This chapter includes ideas and directions for a wide variety of decorative and practical projects. Including wearables, home decorating items, fine paper materials, and gifts. I hope you'll use these projects as a starting point for developing your own creations, as well.

PROJECTS WITH PAPER

Paper lends itself to revealing the beauty of a nature print in a way unlike any other surface. The myriad of textures, colors, and weights of paper provide endless opportunities for using nature printing in many different ways.

Nature-Printed Giftwrap

Decorative giftwrap can be made for any occasion using stamp pads, paper, and leaves. You can also use printmaking inks. Try newsprint, sumi, white butcher paper, or colored kraft paper. For a more special look try decorative and/or textured Asian printmaking papers. All of these papers are available in large sheets or rolls.

The brown kraft paper giftwrapping shown in photo was made with a random pattern of various sized leaves inked with stamp pads. A regular pattern was achieved on the more elegant black giftwrap. This was done by

Nature-printed giftwrap.

French-Fold Notecards, Invitations, & Holiday Cards

A French-fold makes distinctive cards from sheets of standard-size paper. Envelopes for this size card are readily available in stationery stores or in large quantity from your local print shop.

Project Materials

- Good quality 8½-inch by 11-inch stationery or typing paper (or a box of ready-made blank cards purchased from an art and craft supplier, stationer, or local print shop)

- 4⅜-inch by 5¾-inch envelopes to match cards

- Leaf stamping supplies (see page 28) or basic direct method printing supplies (see page 32)

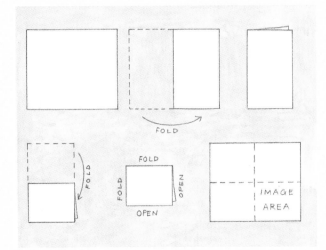

1. Make the French-fold by folding one sheet of paper exactly in half lengthwise, then in half again. Turn the card so the folded edges are at the top and left side. Now the card is right-side up with the front of the card showing.

(**Left**) *French-folded notecards.* (**Right**) *Herbal Wreath, a notecard offset printed from an original nature print by Renata Sawyer.*

2. Open the French-fold and lay the sheet flat so that the top, right-side up section appears on the bottom right square (as shown). Stamp or print your choice of nature-printed images on this square. If you're printing overlapping images, allow each to dry for a short time before printing the next; if you're printing multiple sheets, don't stack them while drying.

3. Print envelopes, if desired (see page 31).

4. When the ink is dry, use markers or pencils to add more color or lettering, if desired. Refold the cards and, if you like, store them in a lidded box that has been sprayed inside with your favorite fragrance or provided with an herbal sachet. These scented cards make special messages to send or give as a gift.

Variation: There's something special about individually hand-printed cards, but for occasions when you need multiple copies of a card quickly technology comes in handy.

Begin by creating a design that you like with black ink only. Your design must be very clear and clean, as any soiled or smudged areas will reproduce on the cards. Hide any blemishes or mistakes with liquid correction fluid. Take your finished print to your local offset print shop. They can do a small run of 50 to 100 or more cards on paper of your choice with matching envelopes.

Costly halftone printing is usually not necessary but if it is, ask to see a proof so you can check that the fine details of your original appear in the reproduction before all the cards are run. Colored inks are available, or you may prefer to have it printed in black ink so you can add touches of color to each card with markers or pencils.

The printer can alter the size of your design to fit the size cards you want or, if possible, you can make the original design to the finished size. Other useful services printers offer are scoring, folding, and typesetting, but to avoid these additional expenses, you can hand letter on your original design and fold the finished cards yourself.

If you need a handful of cards in a hurry, take your design to the nearest photocopier, clean the glass, insert your paper of choice, and print.

printing a large sheet of Yatsuo paper with a nature print rubber stamp (see page 30) and block-printing inks. The stamp was printed twice after each inking, giving the appearance of two shades of ink. Remember that rubber stamps must be washed immediately after using printing inks.

Herbarium or Herbal Section Book

The innumerable pleasures and benefits provided by plants can be equaled only by pouring over publications about them. If you enjoy seed catalogs, fill wildflower and gardening books with notations, and find yourself pressing keepsake leaves and flowers in them, then you will enjoy this project of creating a book about your special plants.

The earliest books have been traced back to 3500 B.C. when the Sumerians of Mesopotamia inscribed stone and clay tablets with cuneiform, the first known written language. The Sumerians planted gardens and wrote herbals. Partially deciphered cuneiform inscriptions reveal herbal charms for curing the sick. From this beginning, the long history of herbals is a fascinating one.

Later, herbals and herbariums from the sixteenth through the nineteenth centuries were often illustrated

Theme Ideas for a Nature-Printed Herbarium

- Collections of gathered wildflowers
- Plants from your garden
- Culinary herbs from the market or garden
- Tree leaves
- Plants found while on vacation

Ideas for Herbarium Elements

- Common and scientific name of each plant
- Description of where plant was found
- Date plant was found
- Any further description of plant's interest or importance

with nature prints. Nature printing historian Peter Heilmann tells us of an Italian aromatarius (spice dealer) named Zenobius Pacinus, well-known for two herbals that are now housed in Paris. When nature printing all the medicinal plants for his famous *ad vitam longam* (remedy for long life), he included the nature print of a viper. Apparently, venomous snakes were an important ingredient in his concoction. In creating your own nature-printed volume, you will be practicing a truly ancient, and sometimes curious, art which has evolved over thousands of years.

An Herbarium is a collection of pressed, dried plants that have been mounted and labeled. Botanists and educators continue to maintain herbarium collections for research and teaching. Botanical gardens, universities, and other institutions painstakingly prepare carefully selected plants. The specimens are flattened in a plant press, mounted on acid free herbarium paper with glue, labeled with a variety of pertinent information, and catalog filed in a controlled environment to last for hundreds of years. Unlike today, nature-printed herbariums were common during the fifteenth through the nineteenth centuries in addition to pressed plant herbariums.

What is Classified as an Herb?

An herb is defined as any plant having a fleshy stem that dies back at the end of the growing season. The word *herb* applies to plants that contain medicinal or cleansing properties or that serve in cooking, perfumery, and dyeing because of inherent flavors, fragrances, and pigments. This includes many plants, indeed. However, there are trees and shrubs that also have some of these properties, for example, juniper, fig, horse chestnut, sassafras, linden, and eucalyptus trees. And shrubs such as senna, elder, wintergreen, and witchhazel serve as herbs do, as well.

Herbals were the first medical books. Written descriptions, often with illustrations, identified each plant with a list of its medicinal virtues. Methods of plant preparation and prescriptions for specific ailments were included. Herbals have recently regained popularity with the resurgence of appreciation of the useful qualities of the plant kingdom. Modern herbals are friendly, all-purpose books containing plant histories and legends, cosmetic and culinary recipes, cultivation techniques, crafts, and all sorts of information.

For inspiration on what to include in your herbal, see *The Country Diary Herbal,* by Sarah Hollis, *The Old English Herbals,* by Eleanour Sinclair Rohde, and *The Herbal or General History of Plants,* by John Gerard (this book is a reprint of an enlarged version of the original, which was published in 1597 and is still one of the most popular Elizabethan herbals). The following are a few thematic suggestions:

- Favorite recipes illustrated with nature-printed fruits, vegetables, and herbs

- Nature-printed blossoms from your perennial bed, accompanied by the flower language of each one

- A nature-printed collection of plants with special significance or of particular interest to you

An Herbal Registry

An herbal or herbarium in the form of a section book is one way to maintain a registry of a plant collection (see following page). Gyotaku, the art of Japanese fish printing, originated as a method for fishermen to record the game fish they caught (see page 50). We can borrow this idea to make a record of garden plants grown.

The herbal print *My Garden Herbs* serves as a registry of the plants in my herb garden. I used water-based inks on printmaking paper to print the herbs. A watercolor wash was then brushed over many of the prints after the ink dried. The herbs are labeled with colored pencils.

An herbal registry: *My Garden Herbs,* 11 inches by 17 inches.

Making a Section Book

*T*hese directions are an adaptation of the basic procedure developed a thousand years ago. Traditionally, the sections are later sewn and bound together to make a larger book. (For additional information on making section books, see the Appendix.)

Project Materials

- Six sheets of 8½- by 11-inch typing paper
- One sheet of heavy paper for the cover cut to size, 8¾-inch by 11¼-inch
- Hand sewing needle and thread
- Ruler
- Pencil
- Scissors

An herbal section book.

1. Fold the six sheets of paper in half, one at a time, short end to short end. Place them inside one another. Fold the cover sheet in half and place around the folded sheets. The cover will be slightly larger than the pages.

2. Open the "book" and center the pages within the cover. Along the inside fold, measure 4¼ inches from one end of the pages to find the center of the fold and make a pencil dot at that point. Mark a dot two inches from both sides of the center dot.

3. Thread the needle with at least a 22-inch length of thread; double the thread and knot the end. Make sure the pages are even around all edges and centered within the cover sheet. Holding the book firmly, make three small holes at the pencil dots by poking the needle through all the paper at each point.

4. From the inside of the open book, push the needle all the way through the center hole and draw the thread through, leaving a 2-inch tail of thread dangling for tying off when the sewing is complete. From the out-

side, push the needle through one of the side holes to the inside and draw the thread through. The 2-inch stitch along the back of the book should be pulled firmly against the fold.

5. Direct the needle through the center hole again and pull through. From outside the book, direct the needle through the other side hole back to the inside. Pull the thread gently from both ends to tighten the stitches. Cut the thread off the needle, tie the cut end and the knotted tail end together in a double knot and trim the excess thread.

Variations: You can adapt this procedure for any size paper you desire or to accommodate the size plants you will be printing but you must always have an odd number of holes for sewing. Try using weighty print-making papers for sheets and heavy art paper or a marbled sheet for a cover.

Instead of using thread, sew a longer piece of ornamental gold or silver cord through the holes starting from the cover; finish with a bow along the cover. Another binding alternative using very sturdy papers is to punch holes in the fold, and tie with yarn or leather stripping instead of thread. Let the ends hang and attach dangling decorative beads.

Nature-Printed Calendar

This nature-printed wall calendar is made from a blank Sketchbook brand calendar, available at art and craft supply stores (see Appendix). The months and days are printed on the bottom half; you supply the nature prints for the top half and the cover. Prints with stamp pads or block printing inks, not watercolors. Be sure to test print your plants on newsprint before printing on the actual calendar.

If you're making gifts, purchase several calendars for the year after the current one, then add nature prints each month as plants bloom or become available — by

Nature printing can be used to make a beautiful, personalized calendar.

December you'll have your gifts ready. Another theme is to use herb nature prints and include an accompanying recipe for an herb dish, potpourri, or other herb craft on each page.

Mixed Media Nature Printing

Try combining nature printing with other media such as watercolor painting, pencil line drawing, and calligraphy.

For Herb Tea, I chose the subjects for the composition — the actual pressed herbs, cut-out sketches of the teapot and cup and saucer, and a torn bit of lace. Then I placed all the objects on a sheet of Arches 140 lb. hot-press watercolor paper and moved them around until I was satisfied with the composition. Once I had my layout, I marked the position of the herbs and lace and then traced my sketches of the tea set on the paper.

I drew the intricate lace with very sharp colored pencils. I painted the traced tea set in watercolor, using a still life set before me for reference. I printed the herbs

Nature printing combined with line and watercolor art.

with watercolor paints, and finished the picture with calligraphy.

PROJECTS WITH FABRIC

The creation of designs on fabric has been practiced for at least four thousand years. Nature printing on cloth was practiced by the Tahitians for untold generations. In the 1700s, the first explorers to the South Sea Islands noted their decorative patterns, which were made by dipping flowers and leaves in red dye and pressing them to tapa-cloth. At that time, fabric decoration by nature printing was already a long-standing tradition in Tahiti.

Nature printing on fabric uses basically the same technique as printing on paper with ink. Any fabric item in the home can be nature-printed — curtains, pillows, table or bed linens, quilts, upholstery, wall hangings, and floor mats. You can make wearables from nature-printed fabrics. If you don't sew, purchase ready-made wearables such as white or solid color T-shirts, sweatshirts, or aprons at a clothing store or local craft supply store. A simple dress or shirt can be patterned or accented with nature printing. Practical articles such as tote bags and laundry bags are great to ornament. Think creatively! There are nature printers who even print ties and socks.

Using Fabric Paint

If you have fabric paints and dyes that you have purchased for other craft projects, experiment with them for nature printing. Different products vary in their performance and application methods.

Fabric Printing with Fabric Paint

*T*his technique can be used on any type of ready-made fabric item or on yardage of fabric that you intend to sew with after printing.

Project Materials

- Fabric paints (such as DEKA brand)
- Textile extender
- Palette, or cups for mixing paints
- Tweezers
- Artist's brushes — soft or bristle
- Ready-made and ironed fabric item
- Waxed paper or cardboard
- Iron
- Leaves or other natural objects
- Soap and water for cleanup

1. If the fabric is washable, wash it before beginning to print to remove sizing. Iron fabric smooth.

2. Place waxed paper or cardboard between layers of fabric (such as inside a T-shirt) to keep paint from seeping to the other layer.

3. Prepare your paints by mixing any colors you want on a palette or in small cups. You can achieve a wide range of hues by mixing. To create pastel shades, mix paint with additional textile extender.

4. Apply paint to plants or other materials you have selected by first dipping your brush in extender and then in paint.

5. Use tweezers to lift painted plants and position them on fabric in desired location.

Artist Helga Wagner of Germany uses DEKA Permanent Fabric paints to nature print bright, bold designs of plants on antique linens.

© Vern Sawyer

Artist Renata Sawyer creates cool gardens on wearables with DEKA paints.

6. Print using pressing methods described on pages 34 to 35. After printing, allow paint to air dry.

7. Heatset paint by applying a hot iron on the opposite side of the fabric for one minute or a warm iron for four minutes.

I've had the most success with DEKA Permanent Fabric Paints, which do not dry thick and rubbery and are available in a selection of brilliant colors and metallics. They are non-toxic, dry cleanable and washable and can be used on any type of fabric except waterproof fabric. If you choose to use these, follow the directions on the label. The paints can be mixed to create a wide range of hues.

Fabric Wall Hangings

There are many different ways to display nature prints made on fabric. The nature print of everlasting pea (shown in photo at right) was made with ink on dress denim and mounted in a 12-inch wooden embroidery hoop purchased at a craft supply store. To do this, center your print over the inner hoop, then place the outer

Fabric Printing with Ink

*T*he same techniques used for printing with ink on paper can be applied to fabric with very satisfactory results.

Project Materials

- Oil-based printing inks with oil for mixing, or water-based inks and water-soluble vehicle (such as Graphic Chemical brand)
- Bristle brushes, brayers, and/or dabbers
- Prewashed and ironed T-shirt or other ready-made fabric item, or yardage of fabric of your choice
- Palette or cups for mixing inks
- Tweezers
- Waxed paper or cardboard
- Leaves or other natural objects for printing
- Clean up materials: solvents for oil-based inks; water and soap for water-based inks

1. If the fabric is washable, wash it before beginning printing to remove sizing. Iron fabric smooth.

2. Place waxed paper or cardboard between layers of fabric if necessary to prevent ink from seeping through to other layers.

Ready-made cotton tote bag and apron purchased at craft supply store and nature printed with water-based inks and vehicle. Lettering done with fabric markers.

3. Follow the directions for preparing and applying ink as described on page 33. You might need to apply a slightly heavier application of ink for heavy or textured fabrics.

4. Ink and print plants as described on pages 33 to 34. Fabric is usable when dry to the touch, but allow ink to set for four weeks before washing fabric.

Fabric wall hangings mounted on small dowel and wooden embroidery hoop.

hoop over it. Pull the fabric gently around all sides to tighten it within the hoop, tighten the screw, and trim the fabric along the edge of the hoop with scissors.

The simple nature print of oak and maple leaves (shown in photo above) was made with ink on silk to be an over-the-door hanging, measuring 8 inches by 32 inches. You can make your own, customized to fit any door.

1. Begin by measuring the space over the door or open entranceway and mark your fabric accordingly. Leave a 1-inch seam allowance along the side and bottom edges so you can fold back the cut edges and stitch them. Alternatively, you can use fuseable tape applied to the cut edge of the fabric with a hot iron. Or, you can eliminate the sides and bottom seam allowances completely by trimming them with pinking shears. Leave a seam allowance of 2 inches across the top to make a sleeve for a dowel.

2. Print the fabric with selected plants arranged in an elongated design.

3. To make the hanger, turn the top 1-inch edge of the fabric over and press. Stitch, turning the bottom edge under ¼ inch. Insert a ⅜-inch wooden dowel into the sleeve. Attach a hook at each end of the dowel and

hang over the door, or tie a decorative cord at both ends and hang from a hook centered over the door. This type of hanging also makes an attractive window valance or trim for a mantle or shelf.

Nature-Printed Patchwork

Anyone talented in needlework may find nature printing fabrics an additional form of self-expression. But you don't have to know how to sew or to cut a straight line to make a nature-printed crazy quilt. Colorful, bold stitches are an easy way of piecing together odd-sized fabric pieces. I enjoyed fashioning this 18-inch by 14½-inch patchwork from brightly patterned cotton blends and nature-printed muslin, silk, and cotton.

Some of the printed leaves were cut out and appliqued onto the center piece of muslin, while others were printed directly onto the quilt fabric. Always make test prints on scrap pieces of fabric first, and remember to save all the successful test prints for appliques.

Crazy quilt. Leaves and flowers nature printed with water-based ink and vehicle on center panel and appliqued onto quilt.

Hammered Print on T-Shirt

*T*his technique doesn't require any paint or ink. Naturally occurring pigments, such as green chlorophyll, are released when a young, juicy leaf is pummeled on natural fiber fabric. The resulting pigmented design is then set in a mineral bath.

Project Materials

- Fresh, young leaves
- Natural fiber fabric, prewashed and ironed
- Hammer with a flat end
- Newspapers
- Waxed paper
- Transparent tape
- Salt or washing soda
- Wood ashes (optional)
- Water
- Iron

1. Lay a section of newspaper topped with a sheet of waxed paper on a hard, flat surface.

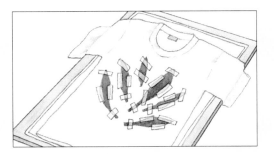

2. Spread the T-shirt on the surface and arrange leaves you intend to print. Secure all edges of each leaf to the fabric with tape. Cover leaves with another sheet of waxed paper.

Hammered-leaf and fabric paint nature prints combined on T-shirt.

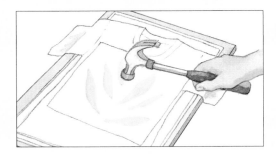

3. Hammer leaves for several minutes until prints appear. Replace the waxed paper cover as needed, if it rips. Some leaves print better than others and coloration will vary. Very fragile leaves disintegrate quickly. You may want to experiment first on a piece of scrap fabric, then select the leaves that work best.

4. To set colorfastness, soak fabric in a solution of ½ cup salt to 2 gallons tepid water for ten minutes, or in a solution of 2 tablespoons washing soda dissolved in 2 gallons tepid water for ten minutes. Rinse thoroughly and dry outdoors or in a dryer. Iron fabric smooth.

Variation: For a reddish-brown color, follow directions in step 4 for a mineral bath and rinse, then immediately soak in 3 gallons of cold water mixed with 1 cup of wood ashes for five minutes. Rinse again, dry, and iron.

PRINTING ON WALLS & FURNISHINGS

Refinishing or touching up furnishings with nature prints is one way to renew your surroundings and to bring nature indoors. Home, deck, and office furniture can be nature printed, including tabletops, chair backs and seats, lampshades, serving trays, filing cabinets, doors, and mouldings. Nature printing also works well on wall surfaces such as wood or painted plaster and dry wall. (Note: Some semi-gloss and enamel-painted surfaces resist nature printing inks. Always make test prints first.) Nature printing can also be combined with stenciling. Nature prints on paper and fabric can be decoupaged onto furnishings or wrapped around them to cover objects such as boxes.

Printing a Wall or Wood Surface

To print on walls or wooden surfaces, you will need all the supplies listed for the basic direct printing method on page 32. Oil-based inks, or water-based inks with water soluble vehicle, work very well on these surfaces and are washable. For added protection on tabletops, apply two coats of polyurethane finish in two to four weeks when nature prints have dried thoroughly. Outdoor furniture requires four coats of polyurethane.

Generally, more ink is needed when printing on painted surfaces than when printing on more absorbent ones such as paper or fabric. To obtain this, roll out a slightly thicker film of ink on the palette with a brayer and coat your selected leaves thoroughly. Expect leaves to produce various results, depending on your chosen printing surface.

Before beginning to print, make test prints on the wall inside of a closet, on a scrap piece of wood, or on a prepared, painted test surface to determine how much ink to apply and to see how the leaves you have chosen will look. Place an inked leaf on your test surface and cover it with a paper towel, a piece of newsprint, or a piece of clear sturdy plastic for better visibility.

Print on your finished surface by hand pressing. For each printing, use a clean cover sheet. The tack of the ink usually helps hold the leaf in contact with a vertical surface, which is helpful when printing on walls. Once finished, remove the leaf with tweezers. Allow several days to two weeks for ink to dry thoroughly before washing (with mild soap and water only).

Variations: If hand pressure is not enough to get a bold print, you may need to apply a heavier application of ink or use another method of applying pressure, such as the following. Once the leaf is somewhat attached to the wall by the tack of the ink and hand rubbing, roll over it with a clean brayer, or use your fist or a rubber hammer to pound all around the leaf with a hammering motion.

This front-porch trunk was not finished with polyurethane to retain its rustic look.

Printing a Regular Pattern or Border

*U*nlike stenciling, nature printing does not lend itself to perfectly symmetric patterns. Even when you carefully register a design on the wall, you can't fully control the distribution of ink as you can when stenciling. And, although sturdy leaves will often make ten or twenty prints, they may break or tear at any time. So, a natural approach to design is most succcessful.

Nature-printed wall border.

1. To create a regular, repeated border choose several leaves of the same kind, alike in size and shape. It's helpful to have about six working leaves and three back-ups.

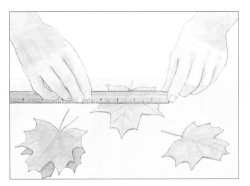

2. Measure the width of each leaf at it's widest point and determine an average width.

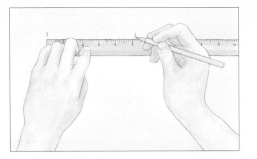

3. Using a ruler, mark this width in light pencil along the wall where you will be printing. Mark a desired margin between leaves of 1 to 6 inches. These are your print registration marks. Center leaves that are slightly larger or smaller than the width marked. When the ink has dried, if any remaining pencil lines show on the wall they can be removed with a kneaded eraser.

When nature printing on a wall, step back occasionally to see how things are progressing. Inconsistencies are fine, as long as they reappear. For example, a lightly inked leaf that didn't print as boldly as the others requires other lightly inked leaves here and there to complement it, or it will look like a mistake.

Variation: For a more complex regular pattern, integrate as many plants as you want into your design, saving a few extras for replacements. Lay the plants on the floor or table to plan your design. A gentle adhesive tape such as drafting or magic tape will hold them in place on the wall to help you view the design before printing it. Mark the location of each with light pencil, remove the leaves, then ink and print. When printing, continue in the same repeating order.

PRINTING PROJECTS FOR CHILDREN

When children make hand prints, apple "star" printing, and potato prints, they are nature printing. Searching for natural objects is as much fun as printing them. Encourage children to go on a nature-printing treasure hunt. They will enjoy finding leaves, flowers, sticks, feathers, shells, seed pods, moss, mushrooms, grass, and rocks and then discovering the images they can make from these objects.

Nature Streaking

Very young children can nature print by simply rubbing leaves and flowers across a piece of plain paper, creating a nature streak from the chlorophyll and other natural pigments in the plants. This act of making marks from leaves is rewarding, especially for preschoolers who are more concerned with the doing than with the finished product.

Be sure children use harmless plants for this project. Avoid poisonous plants such as foxglove, lily of the valley, poinsettia, wormwood and others. Culinary herbs and flowers are safe and have the added bonus of producing abundant fragrances when rubbed.

Nature Copying

Photocopiers present fun projects for children of all ages. To nature print on a copier, have each child arrange selected pressed plants on standard size paper and attach them with clear tape. Put the paper on the copier, and print away. Feathers, insects, sticks, and other flat items can be printed in this way, too. Adjust the copier to a "light print" setting and have the children color in their nature copies with crayons. For children who know their ABC's, have them label the prints they make.

Carbon Paper Printing

Carbon paper (which is still available in stationery and office supply stores, but don't use the smudgeproof kind) deposits its black color when rubbed on leaves. To make a print, simply place a leaf inside a folded sheet of carbon paper and rub on the outside to transfer the carbon to the leaf. Move the leaf to the inside of a folded sheet of newsprint and press or rub the image onto the paper.

Leaf Stamping

Leaf stamps are made with a stamp pad and leaves instead of rubber stamps. These are great fun for both children and adults. See page 28 for complete directions.

Nature Journal

A nature journal makes a great project for a child at scout or summer camp, on a family vacation in the outdoors, or just exploring the backyard at home. Encourage children to include nature prints, photographs, thoughts, a diary of daily camp or vacation events, and observations about the wilderness. See page 37 for directions.

Children will enjoy transforming nature prints into imaginary creatures, as children's book author Irmgard Lucht did in this illustration for **Alle Meine Blatter (All My Leaves)**, *1976.*

Tempera Nature Printing

Many of the nature-printing supplies used by adults, such as oil-based inks, can be used by older children under the supervision of an adult. However, young children should use only nontoxic supplies. While most water-based ink is nontoxic, nature printer John Doughty has developed a simpler method for school and camp groups, using materials that are safe for children, washable with soap and water, and inexpensive.

Tempera paint alone produces poor prints. But John's combination of tempera, honey, and glycerin forms a workable mixture that coats objects evenly and doesn't dry while you're working with it.

Project Materials

- Liquid tempera (Crayola brand, or other good-quality paints)
- Dabbers (see directions for making on page 20)
- Small containers or cups for mixing tempera recipe
- Glycerine (from a pharmacy)
- Honey
- Freezer wrap
- Masking tape
- Tweezers
- Paper (typing, copier, or newsprint)
- Flat leaves (you can flatten curved leaves in a telephone book with weight on top for about thirty minutes)

1. Begin by preparing the tempera paints. For each color, mix eight parts tempera with three parts honey and two parts glycerine.

2. Prepare the workspace. If working outside, keep out of the wind and direct sunlight or the paint will dry too fast. Cover tabletop or other flat surface with newspapers or a washable covering. Tear a sheet of freezer wrap to serve as a palette. Attach freezer wrap corners to the tabletop with masking tape.

3. Place a *few drops* of tempera mixture on the freezer wrap palette. Too much paint on leaves results in a poor print. Use the dabber to thinly spread the tempera on the palette, making an area larger than the leaf you will be printing.

4. Fold a piece of printing paper in half, open it again, and lay it next to the palette.

5. Place a leaf in the middle of the spread tempera and dab the leaf, pressing all around until it's covered with a thin, even coat of paint. Pick up the leaf with the tweezers, turn it over, and repeat paint application on the other side.

6. Pick up the leaf carefully with tweezers and place it on one half of the printing paper. Don't move the leaf once it is on the paper. Fold the other half over the leaf and press on top with the heel of your hand. If the leaf is larger than the heel of your hand, hold the paper down with one hand and press all around with the heel or fingers of the other hand, or use a gentle rubbing motion.

7. Open the folded sheet and carefully remove leaf with tweezers. Notice that double printing doesn't produce a mirror image: Leaf veins are usually more prominent on the underside, showing more detail. If your prints are heavy, too much paint was

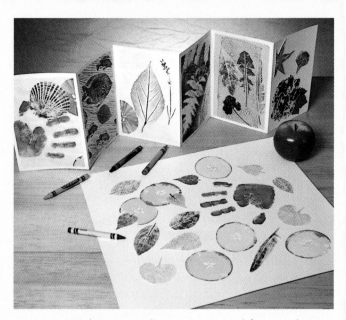

Tempera print by Cara Bethmann, age 7, and free-standing frieze (7¼ inches by 30 inches) by Kate Bethmann, 12, and Cara Bethmann in collaboration with their mother, the author.

used. If they appear pale and vague, use a little more paint.

8. Lay prints flat to dry.

Variation: You might want to make a walking press, which is particularly fun for children (because children have a tendency to jump up and down rather than walk on it). See page 25 for instructions, or simply lay a padding of newspapers on a smooth floor or firm carpet, sandwich the inked leaves and printing paper in between and step upon it, becoming a human printing press!

Tempera prints can be cut out and combined with other media and glued to a three-dimensional free-standing frieze made of sturdy folded paper (see photo).

Bubble Printing

*T*he bubble pattern is found frequently in nature: rushing water, honeycombs, seed pods, and the tiny world of cell structure.

Project Materials

- Mild liquid soap
- Several colors of water-soluble bottled pen ink
- Wide-top containers or jars
- Drinking straws
- Printing paper

1. Set out a container for each ink color. Put 1 inch of liquid soap in each container. Add 1 tablespoon of ink and one straw to each container and mix.

2. Blow through the straw until bubbles come up over the top of the container.

3. Remove the straw and lay a sheet of paper on top of the bubbles. On contact, the pattern will appear on the paper. Repeat process with the other ink colors on the same sheet of paper to make a multicolored design.

4. Thin paper will buckle as it dries. To flatten, apply a warm iron to the dried bubble print. These designs make nice pictures just as they are, or you can add nature prints of leaves and other natural objects.

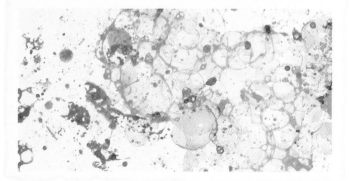

APPENDIX

Organizations

The Nature Printing Society is an international, not-for-profit organization devoted to the artistic and educational pursuit of nature printing. For more information, contact:

> The Nature Printing Society
> Santa Barbara Museum of Natural History
> 2559 Puesta del Sol Road
> Santa Barbara, California 93105

For a sample of the quarterly newsletter, send $1.00.

Mail-Order Suppliers

Daniel Smith
4150 First Avenue South, P.O. Box 4268
Seattle, Washington 98124-5568
1-800-426-6740
Artists' and printmaking supplies, papers, and papyrus. Catalog free.

Dick Blick
P.O. Box 1267
Galesburg, Illinois 61402-1267
309-343-6181
Artists' and printmaking supplies, craft supplies, fabric paints, Sketchbook Calendar, and nature print paper. Catalog $4.

Graphic Chemical and Ink Company
728 North Yale Ave.
P.O. Box 27
Villa Park, Illinois 60181
1-800-465-7382
Printmaking tools, supplies, inks and papers. Catalog free.

Fred B. Mullet (Member of the Nature Printing Society)
2707 59th Street South West, Suite A
Seattle, Washington 98116
206-932-9482
Wholesale and retail nature print stamps, please call during business hours, Pacific time, for information and catalog.

OAS (Oriental Art Supply)
P.O. Box 6596
Huntington Beach, California 92615
714-969-4470
Asian papers and brushes (some not readily available from other suppliers), also seals and chops. Catalog $2.

Further Reading

Agricultural Research Service of the United States Department of Agriculture. *Common Weeds of the United States*. New York, 1971: Dover Publications.

Angel, Marie. *The Art of Calligraphy: A Practical Guide*. New York, 1977: Charles Scribners & Sons.

Cave, Roderick and Geoffrey Wakeman. *Typographia Naturalis,.* Wymondam, England, 1967: Brewhouse Press.

Cook, Theodore Andrea. *The Curves of Life,* New York, 1979: Dover Publications (first published in 1914).

Dolloff, Francis W. and Roy L. Perkinson. *How to Care for Works of Art on Paper.*Boston, 1985: The Museum of Fine Arts.

Geary, Ida. *Plant Prints and Collages*. New York, 1978: Viking Press.

Gerard, John. *The Herbal or General History of Plants* New York, 1975: Dover Publicaions (reprint of version published in 1633).

Holden, Edith. *The Country Diary of an Edwardian Lady*. New York, 1977: Arcade Publishing (originally written in 1906).

Holden, Edith. *The Nature Notes of an Edwardian Lady*. New York,l989: Arcade Publishing (originally written in 1905).

Hollis, Sarah. *The Country Diary Herbal*. New York, 1990: Henry Holt and Company.

Hyder, Max. *Matting, Mounting, and Framing Art — A Practical Guide for Professional Results*.

Johnson, Pauline. *Creative Bookbinding*. New York, 1990: Dover Publications.

The Nature Printing Society. *Printing From Nature: A Guidebook by The NPS*. Santa Barbara, CA, 1992: The Nature Printing Society.

Newcomb, Lawrence. *Newcomb's Wildflower Guide*. Boston, 1989: Little, Brown, and Company.

Pluckrose, Henry. *Bookcraft*. New York, 1992: Franklin Watts Publisher.

Rohde, Eleanor Sinclair. *The Old English Herbals*. New York, 1971: Dover Publications (first published in 1922).

Saddington, Marianne. *Making Your Own Paper*. Pownal, VT, 1992: Storey Communications, Inc.

Snyder, Jill. *Caring for Your Art, A Guide for Artists, Collectors, Galleries and Art Institutions*. New York, 1990: Allworth Press.

Stevens, Peter S. *Patterns in Nature*. Boston, 1974: Little, Brown and Company.

INDEX

Page numbers in italics represent illustrations.

M

Markers, leaf stamping with, 30, *30*

Mounting prints, 69, *69*

Mushroom spores, printing, 53–54, *54*

N

Nature journal
  for children, 85
  how to make, 37, *37*

Nature printing
  defined, 1
  history of, 3–5
  present-day, 5
  uses for, 2

P

Palette, 20

Palette knives, 20, *21*

Paper
  art, 22–23, *22*
  newsprint and sumi, 22
  obtaining desired size, 23, *23*
  sized and watercolor, 39–40, *40*
  terminology, 24

Papyrus, 24

Pencils, use of, 20

Pigment applicators, 20–21, *20, 21*

Pigments, 18–20, *18, 19*

Plant specimens
  equipment for obtaining, 9–10, *9*
  field collecting, 8–10
  leaves for beginners, list of, 8
  observation of, 58–60, *58, 59*
  record keeping of, 10
  sources for, 8
  transporting, 10–11, *10*

Pressing equipment, *10*, 24–25, *25*

Pressing techniques
  cold, 14
  compensating for thick and thin leaves, 12, *12*
  for flowers, 12–13, *13*
  for fruits and vegetables, 14
  for large, flowering plants, 13–14
  remoisturizing dry plants, 14–15, *15*
  for small plants, 11–12, *11, 12*

Printing methods
  alternatives to hand pressure, 35
  direct, 28, 32–38, *32, 33, 34, 35, 36, 37*
  for fruits/vegetables, 48–49, *48*
  indirect, 28
  for large, flowering plants, 44–48, *44, 46, 47*
  leaf stamping, 28–31, *28, 29, 30, 31*
  watercolor, 38–41, *38, 39, 40, 41, 42*

Printing press
  flat bed, 35
  walking, 25, *25*

Q

Quilt, 81, *81*

R

Record keeping, 10

Rolling, 35

Roses, pressing, 13, *13, 68*

Rubber stamps, 30, *30*

Rubbing, 20

S

Seashells and shelled animals, printing and inking, 49–50, *49, 59*

Section book, how to make a, 76–77, *76, 77*

Sized printmaking paper, using, 39–40, *40*

Solvent substitutes, safe, 18

Spider webs, printing, 52–53, *53*

Stamp pads, 28

Stationery
  French-folded, 72–73, *72, 73*
  leaf-stamped, 31, *31*

Stork's-bill, printing of, 44–46, *44, 46*

Sureset, 19

T

Taku-ga, 51–52, *51, 52*, 63

Tamping, 35

Tempera printing, 86–87, *87*

Textile extender, 19

Thermography, 30

T-shirts, hammer printing, 82, *82*

V

Vegetables
  pressing, 14
  printing and inking, 48–49
  watercolor printing of, 41, *41, 42*

W

Walking method of printing, 35

Walking press, how to make, 25, *25*

Wall borders, 84, *84*

Wall hangings, 80–81, *81*

Walls, printing on, 83–84, *84*

Watercolor paint, 19

Watercolor printing, *38*
  dampening paper, 39–40
  equipment and supplies for, 38
  steps for, 39, *39*
  tips for better prints, 40
  troubleshooting, 40
  using sized and watercolor papers, 39–40, *40*
  vegetable prints made by, 41, *41, 42*

OREGANO

QUEEN·ANNE'S·LACE

WORMWOOD

Thym

YARROW

Dyer's CHAMOMILE

ROSE

CHAMOMILE

ENTED
ERANIUM

LADY'S MANTLE